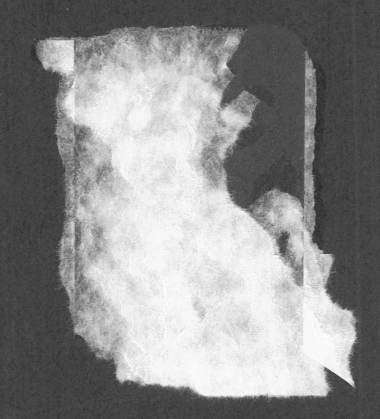

PERILLO

Artist of the American West

ARTIST OF

Perillo

THE AMERICAN WEST

By Gregory Perillo

and Stephen DiLauro

ALPINE FINE ARTS COLLECTION, LTD.
Publishers of Fine Art Books
527 Madison Avenue, New York, New York 10022

Published in 1981 by:

ALPINE FINE ARTS COLLECTION, LTD.
527 Madison Avenue, New York, NY 10022

ISBN: 0-933516-20-7

This book was published in association with Prudential Press, Inc.

This book was produced in Japan.

Designed by Philip Grushkin.

This book was published with the cooperation of Daiichi Seihan
USA, Inc. and Daiichi Seihan Tokyo. Cooperating in the
production of the book were Tomeji Maruyama, President and
William J. Bianco, Vice President. Assisting Mr. Grushkin were
Leo Glueckselig and Laszlo Matulay. Pamela Barr was the editor in
charge of this project. Many of the color photographs were taken
by Eric Pollitzer.

CONTENTS

INTRODUCTION
by Dr. Frederick J. Dockstaeder.

WESTERN ART, as everyone knows, has exploded in recent years. The daily newspapers, magazines, museums and art galleries all testify to this strong interest with overwhelming—if sometimes monotonous—regularity. Much of the work displayed is of superb quality, demonstrating the best that man's aesthetic eye and skilled hand can achieve; some is quite poor and will in time find its own level. The great bulk of Western painting consists of observations, compositions and personal "statements" which provide episodic narrative scenes created to capture a brief moment in life. Many of them are packed to the frames with action, violent and perilous; while an equal number are of subjects caught in quiet repose, serene, restful and sometimes melancholy—but all are relatively simple in their direct appeal to the viewer, tending to refer to an earlier period when life was simpler, if often more brutal.

They are almost universally, by definition, related to a very few major themes: the original nature of the land, its early inhabitants, the entry of the pioneer-settler-exploiter and later occupants, be they farmer or cowboy. It is interesting to note that the white shepherd is rarely painted; the logger occupies small space, and the miner or fisherman appears hardly at all.

Shepherds are usually Indians in a picturesque setting; miners and loggers are puzzling to most Western art buffs, and find a gallery home only in a few localized regions, as do the fishermen. The choice of subjects is extremely biased in favor of the action-packed cowboy-and-Indian theme. And even here, it is largely limited to the people of a specific area and time: the Plains Indians of the brief post-Civil War era.

Of course, the reasons for this are understandable: this is a recent art—its practitioners, while related to the early "action painters" of Old World military scenes, entered the scene less than two hundred years ago, and the great bulk of painters have worked for less than a century. It must be realized that aside from the Spanish explorer-settlers whose horses and cattle started the *genre*, cowboys did not effectively occupy the scene until the late nineteenth century.

But with the coming together of man, horse and cattle, a new artistic terrain developed rapidly—one of a short-lived Golden Age; short-lived because the railroads, fences and highways changed the complexion of the cattleman's existence almost overnight. And this trauma is reflected in the art, which is in essence an attempt to capture the historic past, strongly affected by the exotic landscape and its magnificent changes of color. The painters, many of them refugees from Old World population pressures, found in this last natural beauty an irresistible attraction and challenge; also sensing the world closing in around them, they admired the feeling of freedom offered by the vast areas of the West, just as they were fascinated by its native inhabitants.

From this has come a colorful yet circumscribed art with a surprising loss of freedom exerted by the begrudging dictates of the Western art market and its customers and critics. In generalized terms one can say that it is peopled by a world viewed in romantic terms, replete with stereotype, and painted almost to a formula; yet possessed of a color, vibrancy and action unequaled in most other media.

Sublimation of violent deeds in a peaceful setting is seen in many of the compositions, as is the struggle of Man against Nature. The cowboy is portrayed in many rôles: as a gentleman, knight-in-armor, jester, scruffy hard-working loner, or a jovial, gregarious hard-playing "bunky". The Western soldier or cavalryman is the White Knight protecting the settler, controlling the Indian, and overseeing the traveler across the limitless, hostile landscape. One usually sees the settler as a lone man involved in the unending struggle to win the land, build a home, raise his crops, and defend his family. Rarely are these individuals portrayed in their less admirable—if often equally frequent—lapses from civilized behavior.

The Indian, on the other hand, occupies an unhappy position in most Western art. In actual life he never, or rarely, existed in the mainstream; his knowledge or skills were usually belittled; he was totally ignored socially and politically; and his culture (when it was acknowledged) was regarded as colorful and fascinating but envied by few. Yet he was, after all, the original occupant of the land, and more importantly, he knew where the gold was—which made him of marginal importance if only for the brief time it took to remove him. And this ambivalence shows throughout the art. It is a sophisticated yet surprisingly naive art form, and in dealing with the Indian as a subject, most Western artists treat this as something in the safely dead historical past. His contemporary descendant is more often than not an unpleasant political problem, difficult to handle artistically. The paintings, although often of impeccably accurate ethnographic detail, rarely portray real life. Racism and social chauvinism lie extremely close to the surface, and often appear in unexpected forms. In most Western art, one sees Rousseau's "Noble Savage" personified.

The paradox which haunts many white artists painting the Indian—and few are entirely free from the problem, though some handle it better than others—is the dual image of athletic or admirable Indian as against the lazy, inept or drunken savage. The brave warrior, bold buffalo hunter, or the ineffective loser in Nature's contest all quarrel with one another in the artist's mind. Most Indians painted by the Western artists are essentially the same: one model from the Plains could serve for the vast majority. He is either one who enjoyed an easy life in a primitive Eden, or was faced with a harsh environment in which his culture was unable to cope with the fury of nature.

Out of this taming of man, animal and nature has come an art form which, in no small measure, reflects our own self-image, which in turn grew out of a successful and violent revolution. One can find the antecedents of much of this art in the realistic victory paintings of eighteenth and nineteenth-century Europe; the same spirit of triumph, which, unfortunately, tends to view the rest of the world with scorn, characterizes a good deal of Western painting.

Yet, withal, some of these regrettable attitudes have yielded an exciting visual expression replete with historic characters, colorful landscapes, super-active episodes and emotionally-arousing narrative qualities. Much of it is wholly imaginative and often gives a sense of unreality, while other compositions mirror life in an incredibly precise and "perfected" manner. Indeed, part of the charm of Western art is this black-and-white, day-and-night, good-or-bad absolute which is so frequently embodied in the work.

The degree of precision creates another consideration: the old argument of photography *versus* painting, in which the world as seen by man competes with the world as seen by the camera. In this contest, the verdict is not yet in: but it will probably result in a draw. The artist can take liberties with what he sees in order to provide an interpretation, emotion or emphasis; the camera enjoys this luxury to a more limited degree. Yet no artist can record actuality to the finite degree provided by the photographer as easily and quickly. Before photography, the artist was the sole recorder of the passing scene, and we are today at the mercy of the historical, social, or political feelings of the early artist, if not his skill. Much of the subtlety of a scene is more effectively rendered by the brush than the lens, particularly where color or movement is involved. And the artist has one other advantage over the photographer: in his compositions he can eliminate or include elements according to his will.

It is into this world that Gregory Perillo entered, and has remained since his early boyhood. The accompanying text to this volume clearly demonstrates how neatly he fits into this paradoxical pattern: he is a complete Easterner of mixed Euro-American extraction, with a background which has undoubtedly had considerable cultural impact upon his attitudes towards his art, if not the work itself. He is a sensitive, emotional man who responds quickly to the world in which he lives, blessed with skilled hands and a sharp eye for detail. His reactions to the land beyond the Mississippi, its Indian inhabitants, and the activities of the various occupants, white and Indian, also clearly show in his work. He has a vivid sense of color, good feeling for composition, and a fine grasp of anatomy. All of his work has the strong "you are there" characterization.

Perillo enjoys action and portrays it well, demonstrating a powerful sense of emotion towards his narrative scenes, as well as the participants. Often this is strengthened by great vitality, while at other times it can be tremendously romantic and tranquil. His more recent *Companions* series betrays this emotional relationship dramatically. A willingness to experiment is responsible for his exploration into sculpture and bronze casting, in which he has been extremely successful. It is interesting to note that he is one of the few Western artists who rarely features the cowboy in his work.

What does not come through as readily in his narrative is the actual degree of intimacy which he has enjoyed with his Indian models; the elements of his life which have enabled him to act as an interpreter of that world are obscure, as are something of his inner feelings about much of it. Working in his studio, as do most Western painters, he suffers from the great distances between Staten Island and his chosen region perhaps more than those painters residing in the Western states, but his sketchbooks, memory and photographic records have gone far to overcome this handicap, strengthened by annual visits to the Indian country to pick up details. Surprisingly, unlike many of his colleagues, Perillo does not have a large collection of Indian objects in his studio.

Recent changes of attitude toward the art would have been rewarding to the entire field: whereas precise or "realistic" art was out of favor for many decades, there has been a dramatic return to the more literal style; and today, *trompe l'oeil* is finding increasing numbers of practitioners who enjoy gallery shows impossible to obtain ten years ago. Museums are equally active in welcoming back an earlier art form which had lain unseen in storage vaults, and the approval of the Establishment is manifest in the creation of special "Western Art" galleries in many museums. The number of galleries handling only Western art has expanded tremendously—these exist now in almost every city in the country, each with a strong complement of collectors. Interest in Europe and Japan has also helped in creating a strong market which one feels will only increase as more and more collectors enter the field—and the world re-created for us by the Western artist recedes even farther into the historic past.

Exhibition at
Wally Findlay Gallery,
57th Street, New York.

Perillo painting
Chief Victoria.
Painting of Chief Joseph
in background.

Chief Big Tree
and nephew
with Perillo.

Perillo
on horseback.

THE GREETING

1

The Making of a Western Artist

FOR AS LONG as I can remember the American West has fascinated me. As a child in Staten Island, New York, I spent many hours at the library poring over books which depicted the vastness and grandeur of America west of the Mississippi. It was also through reading that I learned about the tragic history of the original citizens of this continent. Many years lapsed between these childhood researches on Staten Island and the time when I was finally able to visit the areas that became a lifelong source of inspiration for me.

It was in 1949, while serving in the United States Navy, that I had my first look at the American West, thanks to one of my shipmates. After I showed him some sketches I had done while we were out at sea, he asked me if I had ever seen any real cowboys and Indians. "Only in the movies," I told him. He was from Montana and it turned out that his father owned a ranch there. A number of the cowhands were Blackfeet Indians, and he invited me to join him on a trip out there the next time we could get leave.

We hitchhiked our way up into Montana in less than thirty-six hours. It was my first time ever in such wide open spaces and I was simply astounded at the breathtaking beauty of it all.

We were standing alongside a county road with our thumbs out when an old tin lizzy Ford stopped. We scrambled into the back seat. There they were—my first real live Indians. The man was dressed in Levis with a cowboy hat. His hair was in long thin braids that fell past his shoulders. The woman was heavy-set and wearing something that looked like a bed sheet. For about the first ten minutes she kept staring at me and giggling, not saying anything. When she finally did speak she laughingly asked me to forgive her poor manners. "It's just so funny to see an Indian with curls," she said. "I've never seen it before. What tribe are you from?"

That was the first time I was mistaken for an Indian. It has happened again over the years, with both my "paleface brothers" and with other Indians as well. These mix-ups have put me in some interesting situations.

It was this first trip out West that enabled me to put a painting like *The Red Prize* on canvas years later. Sketching cowboys, cattle on the range, horses on the run, Indians—it was all a revelation.

Plate 1

The impact of a painting like *The Red Prize* lies in the action. The clouds of dust rising behind the stampeding mustangs open up the scene, allowing its power and tension to show through, as in the bunched muscles of the cowhand's pony. Contrast this image with the wild, red mustang at the center of the scene. The mustang is calm, loping along, unaware of the impending tightening and yanking of the lariat. It is a young horse and behind the whole scene of action lie still mountains. These two symbols, the young wild pony and the eternal mountains, show nature's powers. Man may try to tame the earth, but he will never have more than a piece of it. Nature is always continuing without struggle. The herd of wild horses are a constant reminder that no matter how hard man, represented by the mustachioed cowboy, works to control and dominate the world around him, regeneration will continue. Nature is as old as the mountains and as young as a fast pony.

PLATE 1:
THE RED PRIZE (1973), 24 x 32"
Collection Dr. Michael B. Klein

*In an action painting like this, the most important thing
is to capture the spirit.*

CHEYENNE BRAVE (1972), 30 x 24"
Prudential Collection

I tried to paint this young Cheyenne as his great-grandfather must have looked a hundred years ago, full of ambition and pride.

Whether or not I would have discovered myself as an artist without this first trip out West is a moot point. The fact is that my life was forever changed by that journey. Still, my love of the West, as great as it was and is, could not by itself, or even with the addition of natural talent, have made me into a Western painter. For this I have to thank my good fortune in having had the privilege to study with one of the greatest Western artists of this century, William R. Leigh.

I met Leigh on my first trip out West with my wife, Mary, who I married shortly after my discharge from the navy. We were in a little pueblo in Arizona and I was sketching some Indians in the village square. Across the square from me an older man was also hard at work sketching. When I finished I went over to take a look at what he was working on.

"Hey, you're great," I said as I looked at his drawing of several Navajo women sitting and talking. He looked up from his pad and smiled. Then I recognized him. "Hey," I almost shouted, "you're William R. Leigh." He seemed to get a kick out of the fact that I used his full name.

I had spent hours and hours looking at his work in the Grand Central Art Gallery in New York City and had several times caught a glimpse of the man himself. Now here I was thousands of miles away from home and face to face with a man whom I had never before had the nerve to speak with.

He asked to see my work and as he flipped through my sketchbook he kept nodding to himself. "You're not bad for a kid from New York," he said with a grin. "Why don't you come

PLATE 3:
COWBOYS IN THE RAIN (1975), 24 x 32″
Collection Mr. Shelly Marks

PLATE 4:
BLACKFOOT (1969), 20 x 16″, pen and ink
Prudential Collection

The traditional headdress and ornaments are still worn by the Blackfeet on ceremonial occasions.

PLATE 5:
CHEYENNE (1969), 20 x 16″, pen and ink
Collection Mr. Michael Frost

This heavily lined face shows both the great suffering and the great strength of the Cheyenne people.

and visit me in my studio when I get back in the city?" He gave me his address and I ran off to find Mary and tell her what had happened.

Driving back, Mary had to keep telling me to slow down, I was so excited. It really did not matter how fast I went because Leigh had told me that he would not return to the city for two more months. But I couldn't help myself, I kept speeding up the car, as though that would make the day when I visited his studio come faster.

It was with apprehension that, two months later, I ascended eleven floors in the elevator to visit Mr. Leigh in his studio at 200 West 57th Street in Manhattan. He did not recognize me immediately. But when I reminded him of the circumstances under which we met, he said, "Oh yeah, the kid from New York. You still drawing, kid?" And that was what he always called me—"Kid."

While he went over a book of my latest sketches—I had asked him for some criticism, though what I was looking for was really some sort of approval from a man I considered a master—I marveled at the collection of Western memorabilia he kept around his studio. Navajo saddles, silver bridles, bits and pieces of turquoise jewelry, beaded moccasins, buffalo skulls, skulls of Bighorn rams, pottery bowls and jugs, rugs, blankets, baskets, eagle feathers, all these and more surrounded me. There were Indian quivers and arrows and white men's guns. He even had some sagebrush in his studio. Leigh had a passion for authenticity. He was a perfectionist, noted as one of the most schooled artists in the field of Western lore. His library was composed of hundreds of books on the subject and he referred to it constantly, as I found out later on.

My lessons with Mr. Leigh usually lasted about an hour. They consisted of my working and his criticizing. He was a man of few words. He would tell me to go light on the detail. In those days I used very fine, pointed sable brushes. No matter how many times he told me, it seemed I could not help myself. There was too much detail in my work for Mr. Leigh's liking. Finally one day he could stand it no longer. He took all my sable brushes and broke them in two. Then he gave me six hard, flat-bristle brushes and told me to use those instead.

Though these brushes felt strange in my hand I continued to use them and in several weeks the results became evident: there was just enough detail, not at all overdone. Even Mr. Leigh complimented me a little on the difference.

He also had me constantly draw from life. Leigh's theory was that if one looks at a three-dimensional subject and puts it on a flat suface, one is bound to capture some of the depth and form. But if one draws from a flat surface, such as a photograph, the result will be a flat drawing. He told me that when I became a professional artist I could use a photograph and by that time I would know how to interpret the life in the photo and capture it. But while I was his student he insisted that I draw from life.

One time Leigh invited me to go with him to Central Park. I took the day off from work and we went. I was proud to be there with him. We went to the zoo to sketch the animals. After I did about six of these drawings Leigh told me to do some trees.

PLATE 6:
SIOUX (1969), 20 x 16"
Prudential Collection

This noble Sioux wears an expression that could be anger or mistrust—both would be more than justified.

PLATE 7:
APACHE (1969), 20 x 16", pen and ink
Collection Mr. Daniel Iatvro

Indian faces lend themselves exceptionally well to pen and ink drawings; they are so full of strong lines and curves.

Knowing that this was one exercise I could not stand, he told me
to paint the trees in watercolors and I would enjoy myself.

At times Leigh would leave for a month or two. Upon his
return I always had plenty of work ready for him to look at. He
would take, say, an oil painting I had done and put it on his easel.
As he told me my mistakes he would pick up a brush and paint
right over what I had done wrong.

One afternoon I was working on a painting of a cowhand
shooting at some cattle rustlers. The cowboy had a six-shooter in
his hand. When Leigh saw the painting, his first comment was,
"The gun looks lost." With his thumb he smudged some white
paint from the cowboy's shirt and touched the tip of the barrel
of the gun. The white made the gun jump out, and immediately
catch the eye. It was so simple.

I did not see Mr. Leigh in the latter part of 1952 because he
was busy accepting honors and lecturing. The very last time we
met he told me to keep away from detail and keep on drawing. A
few years later I heard that he had passed away. I felt crushed. I
had lost a friend and teacher.

I remember that he was always telling me to sketch fast. This
is what would enable me to capture the "spirit." His horses,
especially, were always full of life, and he was quite critical of
mine. It seemed I could never do a horse right; there were always
so many faults Mr. Leigh would pick out.

Before long I began to hate to paint horses because I saw all
the same faults that Mr. Leigh did. Yet I knew that I couldn't
very well be a Western painter without being able to do a good

PLATE 9:
SIOUX SCOUT (1978), 42 x 34"
Collection Mary Perillo
*He could be tracking an enemy or searching for traces of his
lost party. The forbidding mountains emphasize his isolation.*

horse. So I started to go to the stables whenever I could, the same
stables where I had drawn as a boy, and practice. I told Mr. Leigh
that when I drew one good enough to paint I would show it to
him.

Finally I painted a horse that I felt I could be proud of. When
it was finished I took it with apprehension to Mr. Leigh. He
looked it over and turned to me. "So, you think it's good?" he
asked.

"Yes," I answered. "I do think it's pretty good. Don't you?"
He did not answer. He studied the painting a bit more and then
gave me a few pointers on a few things I had missed.

"So tell me, kid, why do you think this is a good painting?"

"Because it has spirit, Mr. Leigh. And you always told me
that if you capture the spirit you have succeeded."

He let loose with a great, deep laugh. When he had stopped
laughing he said, in his booming baritone voice, "Yes, Greg, it *is*
a good painting and it does have spirit. Now all you have to do is
work on the anatomy to go with the spirit and you will have
something."

An example of William R. Leigh's influence on my early
work can be seen clearly in *Cowboys in the Rain.* Obviously the *Plate 3*
rain serves to eliminate detail, thus giving the painting the sort
of impressionistic quality Leigh was so fond of. The cowboys are
hunched up and hunkered down in the saddle to protect
themselves as best as possible against the elements. The grass, the
gray sky, the boulders, even the men themselves, are clearly
recognizable without being highly delineated and fiercely

PLATE 10:
NAVAJO MUSTANGS (1972), 24 x 30″
Collection Dr. Michael Paglia

*Rounding up these spirited, wary animals
was a dangerous and difficult job.*

detailed. It is in the horses that realism forces its way into the picture.

Through the anatomy of the horses the viewer of this painting begins to realize that, in spite of the lack of other details, this is in fact a very realistic portrayal of what it is like to see a landscape through the rain.

Forms are always shifting and changing, sometimes imperceptibly, as when light or a breeze plays upon an object, and sometimes through actual motion. The result is that one comes to realize that there is no *one* reality. For a realistic painter this presents the great problem of choice. Whether it is in a stop-action, so to speak, as in *The Red Prize*, or in a painting like *Cowboys in the Rain* where the action seems to flow on, the artist is always faced with the fact that the moment depicted is part of an endless series of moments. Reality is in truth an elusive fantasy. As a realistic artist I come to grips with this fact every morning as I approach my easel. It is the greatest challenge to find the right moment which best expresses the reality sought after. A glimpse of truth is the heart of any realistic painter's work. The events leading up to and following that momentary glimpse must be inferred by the viewer.

For example, whether the viewer sees these cowboys as beginning a day in the saddle, or ending one, is a highly subjective, personal judgement. The objective truth is that rain has slowed down the riders. The painting will tell a slightly different story to everyone who sees it, yet, of course, there are clues. The rope on the first rider's saddle states emphatically that cattle play an important part in the lives of these men. The

PLATE 11:
INDIAN SCOUT (1960), 24 x 18"
Prudential Collection
*The warrior scout is a theme I returned to several times,
as in* Sioux Scout *of 1978, which has a much different feeling.*

blanket roll behind the saddle of the second rider tells part of the story. These are men used to sleeping out of doors. Whether or not one of them is the foreman, or even the ranch owner, would be up for questioning here, because the rain is an equalizing force. Nature is the narrator of this reality. The rain is washing away the hoofprints of the cowboys' mounts almost as fast as they are imprinted on the earth. Once again the message here is that nature is unalterable.

Through my relationship with William R. Leigh I came to know Ruth Raile, who was the assistant director of the Grand Central Gallery. Ruth Raile and Mr. Leigh tried to get me accepted as a member of the gallery, but for some reason the director turned me down. Even so, Miss Raile arranged for one of my paintings to be hanging at all times in the gallery. So I began to sell regularly. Still, I could not support myself solely on the money I was making as an artist. I took various jobs to keep the money coming in, and Mary worked regularly.

At one point things seemed very bad financially. I was out of a job and Mary was pregnant. She told me not to worry, that something would come along. Then she asked whether I wanted a boy or a girl. I told her it didn't matter.

A few weeks later the moment came, we were on the way to the hospital, and I told her that if I had a choice I would have the baby be a boy.

I was too nervous to wait at the hospital. So I went to a hardware store and bought a can of blue paint and went home to

paint the baby's room. When I opened the can, it was *pink* paint.
I had no doubt then that I would be the father of a baby girl,
which is exactly what happened.

Mary was right about my finding a job. A couple of weeks
after Annette was born I got a job working for the Parks
Department. It was perfect for me because it left me with
enough energy to paint after work was over, and with enough
time to visit the galleries and the Museum of Natural History,
where I worked sketching to strengthen my sense of anatomy.

I was depressed about the fact that I could not get a gallery to
represent me. To cheer myself up I did a large painting of Chief
Sitting Bull which was so good, I felt, that I wrote and offered it
to the Pettigrew Museum in Sioux Falls, South Dakota, which is
the heart of Sitting Bull's nation. They accepted it and I was
overjoyed.

Still I was not represented by any gallery, other than the
Grand Central, and technically I was not a member there. Then
one day I was working in Battery Park and I saw an artist looking
out over the harbor and working on a canvas. I strolled over and
took a look. "Hey, that's good," I told the man.

"Can't you see I'm working," he responded, looking up from
the painting of tugboats. "Why don't you get lost."

That was it, the final straw: not only were the galleries
rejecting my work, but now the artists themselves were spurning
me. I mumbled something nasty and barely intelligible under
my breath and walked away. He came running after me and
apologized. Was I a painter, he wanted to know. I answered that I

PLATE 13:
CRACK OF DAWN (1980), 38 x 50″
Collection Mr. and Mrs. John Genna

The tradition of fetching water is an essential part of Navajo life.
The setting is Monument Valley.

PLATE 14:
TIGERS OF THE PLAINS (1960), 31 x 35½″
Collection Arnold M. Chernoff

The Blackfeet were renowned as some of the finest horsemen ever to ride the Great Plains.

was a Western painter. He asked if I was represented by any galleries and I told him no, but if he wanted to see my work he could go to a certain office furniture store on Beaver Street and see some of it there. He asked for my telephone number and said he would go see my work. His name was Bill Lawrence.

That same evening he called me at home and was very complimentary. He offered to sponsor me into the Hudson Valley Art Association. Well, I guess this is how it all got started.

I was accepted as a member of the Association and they published one of my paintings in their magazine, which is mailed to galleries all over the country. Then I won the Connally Award for best pen and ink drawing in 1964. This led to the G. Harvey Gallery in Austin, Texas asking to represent me. This was followed by a similar request from a gallery in Turkey Creek, Colorado. Things were really starting to happen. I worked harder at my art, harder than ever before.

The following year I won an award for painting in a competition sponsored by a Wall Street brokerage firm. My entry is not reproduced here, but it is similar to a later painting entitled *Madre*, which is a sort of nonsecular exploration of the Madonna and Child theme. It shows a Navajo mother holding her papoose, and gives an example of the effect another of my early jobs, as a painter for a studio that specialized in icons and religious murals for churches, had on my painting. During this period my boss, or maestro if you will, was an old Italian man named Zambone. I worked under Mr. Zambone for eighteen months and it was an important time of growth. My sense of depth of field, perspective, and "feeling" were greatly enhanced.

Plate 19

43

CLAY BASKETS (1979), 30 x 24"
Courtesy Empire Art Gallery, Empire, Colorado
Pottery is another traditional craft still practiced by the Navajo today.

The time I have spent with the Navajo tribe in the Southwest was also an influence on the painting of *Madre,* as well as on other paintings such as *Crack of dawn; Weavers;* and *Clay Baskets.* These last three might fall into a category of narrative that might be called "slice of life." *Crack of Dawn* is a look at a daily ritual for the Navajos which still goes on today. Because of the high temperatures of the desert land where they live, tribe members go to the waterhole each morning before the sun rises. I have attempted to give my interpretation of what it was like some one hundred years ago. Though going to the waterhole early in the day is still necessary, it is more likely that someone observing this today would see the water-carriers arrive in a pick-up truck, rather than a wagon.

Plate 13
Plate 12
Plate 15

Weavers is an experiment in viewing daylight from a darkened place. This scene from the daily life of the women and children is shown looking out from the hogan. The hogan is the earthen hut which still serves as the dwelling unit for many of the Navajo who live on the reservation.

Over the years I have spent a lot of time living with the Indians in different parts of the United States. Obviously it has helped my ability to portray their facial features and the details of their day to day existence. I have been honored to know the warmth, exuberance, kindness and nobility of these people. When one comes face to face with their humanity, one cannot help but feel a little ashamed at the history of inhumanity with which our government has treated these original inhabitants of America.

PLATE 16:
BLACKFOOT BRAVE (1966), 30 x 20″
Collection Western Publications,
Austin, Texas

*The anatomy of a horse,
one of my favorite subjects,
is among the most difficult
things the Western painter
has to master.*

PLATE 17:
ARAPAHO (1979), 16 x 20″
Collection Mr. Gus L. Constatinides

*A character study from life of an
Arapaho Indian in Colorado.*

PLATE 18:
ABUELA (1980), 24 x 30"
Courtesy Small World Gallery, Scottsdale, Arizona

A Navajo grandmother—"abuela" in Spanish. The cultural give-and-take between the Navajo and the Mexicans is reflected in their language and clothing.

PLATE 19:
MADRE (1977), 32 x 24"
Courtesy Vague Shadows, Ltd.

I tried to embody the essence of motherhood in this portrait of a Navajo mother and child.

PLATE 20:
SHEPHERD (1979), 24 x 30″
Collection Mr. and Mrs. Richard Cibelli

*Navajo children learn at a very young age how to care
for animals and take on responsibility.*

PLATE 21:
NAVAJO BOY (1980), 16 x 20″
Courtesy Small World Gallery, Scottsdale, Arizona

*I was particularly struck by this child's face—
angelic and impish at the same time.*

PLATE 22:
THE BREED (1961), 24 x 17½″
Collection Arnold M. Chernoff

The Navajo and the Mexicans often shared blood as well as a language.
This half-breed clearly shows features of both races.

PLATE 23:
THE SENTINEL (1959), 24 x 18"
Collection Mr. and Mrs. R. Bricker

A Blackfoot warrior on the lookout for enemies,
carrying the white man's modern tools of warfare.

PLATE 24:
SQUAW TRAVAIS (1958), 25 x 37"
Collection Mr. Donald A. MacDonald

*An ingenious mode of transportation
for the wounded and the weary.*

PLATE 25:
FRANK SMITH, SIOUX (1970), 16 x 20″
Collection Miro Salva

*I spend a lot of time with the Sioux out West, getting to know
them and maybe even to understand them a little.
Frank Smith was one of my favorite models.*

Perillo © 80
COWBOY JOE

2

The Wild West

I HAVE BEEN GOING to Monument Valley, in the northeast part of Arizona and southeastern Utah, for about thirty years now. It is a place of beauty like no other in the United States. The red sandstone buttes, mesas and arches led the movie director John Ford to use this panorama as a backdrop for a number of his finest Westerns.

Whenever I am out that way I am up before the sun so as to have my easel set up when the sun rises. Both the dawns and sunsets there contain colors that simply do not exist anywhere else in the world, not that I know of, anyway. I use a very brash palette—purples, tangerine, lavenders, oranges, several yellows and blues—while working there.

One of the best examples of the inspirational effect the natural wonder of Monument Valley has on my work is the painting *Lonesome Cowboy*. People have accused me of fantasizing the colors in this painting, saying they are too bright to be real. I can only respond that they must go there and see for themselves sometime.

Once in a while, in the West, there is a perfect moment that you just want to capture and put in your pocket so that every so often you will be able to take it out and hear it and see it again and again. It was this sort of moment that I experienced one sunrise in Monument Valley, as the howls of coyotes pierced the stillness. I tried to capture it again in my painting *Lonesome Cowboy*. There is just a hint of a wry grin on the face of this saddle tramp. He knows that it has been who knows how long since he was with a woman or since he had the comfort of a bath. His bed the night before was his blanket and the hard ground,

Plate 27

with a sky full of stars as his roof. He is not concerned with the sandstone monuments carved by time and prehistoric tremblings of the earth. He's seen that horizon a hundred times before. But the yipping and howling of a family of coyotes crooning at the sunrise captures his attention and emotions. He can almost smile at his situation. Hell, he thinks, nobody made me be a cowboy. I did it all on my own.

Another painting that explores this same theme of a cowboy coming to a sort of poetic awakening is *Golden Horizon*. Here, the setting is a corner of the Grand Canyon.

Plate 26

In 1953 I saw the Grand Canyon for the first time. Mary and I had driven all day and finally arrived around midnight. It was magnificent, the night blacker than black, lit up only by the stars so big they seemed close enough to grab. I got out of the car and ran up to the edge of the canyon and stopped just in time. I looked down, my heart went to my throat, followed by my stomach, which leapt to my chest. One more step and it would have been bye-bye Perillo. My legs were frozen and I could not move for about three full minutes. Finally I composed myself and stepped back gingerly from the abyss and returned to the car. Needless to say, Mary decided to wait until morning for her viewing of the canyon. The only other time I ever experienced a feeling like that was the first time I rode the roller coaster at Coney Island.

That night I had a hard time sleeping, I was so excited at the prospect of being able to paint the Grand Canyon. I was up with the birds to take my easel, canvas and paints to the edge.

I found a ledge about seven feet wide, set myself up, sat down

PLATE 26:
GOLDEN HORIZON (1968), 26 x 38″
Collection Dr. and Mrs. James Budd

*Here I tried to re-create the same sense of wonder
I felt when I first beheld this landscape.*

PLATE 27:
LONESOME COWBOY (1980), 38 x 50"
Prudential Collection

The glory of the sunset in Monument Valley can't cure the cowboy's lonesomeness, but it's one of the rewards of his job.

on a small stool and began to paint. I was so engrossed that the hours passed like minutes. All of a sudden, when I was almost finished with my first painting, there came a gust of wind that knocked down my easel. I jumped up and grabbed for my canvas. As I did I looked down. Here I was moving like a welterweight and I was a thousand or more feet up. It was frightening. I looked away, then could not resist glancing back down there. When I did, I let go of the canvas and it went sailing off. I decided to call it a day at that point.

Of course the West was, and still is, much more than landscapes and sunrises, as magnificent and moving as they are. Primarily it was a place filled with action—bronc busting, cattle driving, riding, hunting and fighting. Many of my action paintings portray representative aspects of Indian or cowboy life. Others tell an individual story. The paintings in both of these categories can be called narratives.

Plate 37
Plate 39
Plate 38

In the first category I would place such paintings as *Pony Express, Bronco* and *Day in the Saddle.* They portray everyday events that are anything but commonplace to a man like me. I was raised on Staten Island and things like subways, buses, taxis and jet airplanes overhead are the modes of transportation that have surrounded me all my life. Until I went out West, horseback riding was something rich kids did in the park. The thrill of seeing men at work on horseback has stayed with me since my first stay on the Anderson ranch in Montana. I still enjoy watching cowhands moving through a herd of longhorns, or breaking a spirited horse.

Among my action paintings with "plots" I would classify

Horse Thief, *Side by Side* and *Dead Aim-Southwest*. *Horse Thief* shows a swift-riding Indian leading a string of ponies. We know they are stolen because we see three riders, from a rival tribe, in hot pursuit. From the dust the thief is kicking up we can suppose that he is too fast for them.

Plate 44
Plate 31
Plate 32

Side by Side and *Dead Aim-Southwest* are both outlaw stories. I placed them together here because they portray the same basic protagonists in two opposite situations. In *Side by Side* the outlaws are mounted. They are running from a posse but it is still a long way to the mountains where they have a chance of hiding. There is no cover on the open plain and their horses are spent. They know that their only chance is to stop, to turn, and make a last stand.

In *Dead Aim-Southwest* the tables are turned. The outlaws have barricaded themselves inside an outcrop of boulders. They are sighting their prey in the distance, making sure that when the time comes their shots will count. In this kind of ambush the element of surprise is everything. If the first shots miss their marks they may not have another chance. The tension of the scene is offset by the horses grazing peacefully in the background.

Perhaps my most important narrative painting dealing with the old West, in terms of tension and drama, is *The Slade Gang*. A meaner bunch of outlaws never rode the Southwest. What I have done here is take the theme of a "Last Supper" and place in it the worst, most scurrilous sort of men. The traitor here is obviously the figure at the left in the foreground—a half-breed Indian with feathers in his hair and white man's clothing. He

Plate 28

PLATE 28:
THE SLADE GANG (1973), 34 x 50″
Prudential Collection

A band of outlaws, a confrontation.
The faces and gestures tell the story.

PLATE 29:
STAGECOACH (1960), 18 x 24″
Collection Charles D. Parker

My variation on one of the immortal themes of the Wild West.

was the tracker who was to lead the gang through some pretty bad country and away from the posse that was pursuing them. But after two days on the trail the leader—at the center, with his coffee cup raised to take a sip—has realized that the half-breed has betrayed them. Having called out the Judas among them, all the others have focused their attention on him.

The man with the cap and blond hair and beard is obviously an immigrant, as were many of the early outlaws. I garbed him in European-style clothing to bring out this point. The other half-breed, at the rear and standing, is part of the plot that led to the demise of the Slade gang. But the others have not yet realized this. Each of the men's faces portrays a different emotion: the leader—realization; hate in the man at the right in the foreground; fear is in the eyes of the immigrant; the man standing behind the European is cold as metal and ready to kill—he is amorality personified; the hombre just behind the leader, with the horse behind him, shows contempt. The standing half-breed is duplicity and the one sitting, with only half his face showing, is cowardice. The high barren rocky ground has divested the men of a background. They have come from nowhere to achieve their death.

I wouldn't want to give the impression that all the white men in the Wild West were either cowboys or outlaws. One of the most intriguing men of the West was Christopher "Kit" Carson, who could rival any Indian in his knowledge of the American wilderness. My character study of him hangs in the Pettigrew Museum along with the portrait of *Sitting Bull* with beaver fur wrapped in his braids. Mountain man, trapper, explorer,

Plate 8

PLATE 30:
KIT CARSON (1961), 24 x 18"
Courtesy Pettigrew Museum, Sioux Falls, South Dakota

*Kit Carson was one of the few men who went west
in search of more than just riches and adventure. In this
painting I tried to capture his nobility and wisdom.*

linguist—he spoke French, Spanish, and several Indian dialects,
in addition to his native English—mule skinner, saddle maker,
Indian agent, adventurer extraordinaire and rancher, Kit Carson
felt the explosive force of man and nature coming together on
the frontier. He rode the resulting eruptions like a man busting a
bronc. And the West was tamer after a man like Carson rode it.

I painted *Kit Carson* in 1961. The somber dark green of the
background is something I have since moved away from. I still
enjoy doing character studies and portraits of Indians. I used this
somber tone to create a mood that captures Carson's quiet
heroism.

When you contrast the nobility of Kit Carson's face with the
range of personality portrayed in *The Slade Gang,* you can get a
sense of the disparate forces that were at work in the old West.
For every man who went West with a desire for knowledge of the
continent—such as Kit Carson, or John C. Fremont, who Carson
aided in exploring and mapping the country that lay between
New Mexico and California, or even Lewis and Clark—there
were ten others who went West with greed in their hearts.
Common folks like the pioneers and settlers looked to the noble
men for leadership, and often found themselves at the mercy of
characters like the Slade Gang. The American Indians,
unfortunately, suffered deprivation at the hands of both those
filled with greed and a lust for gold, and those who went West
with the hopes of bettering their lives through the hard work of
settling the land.

Plate 30

PLATE 31:
SIDE BY SIDE (1970), 25 x 33"
Collection Arthur Gladstone

Covering against an attack. We can't see the enemy, and I think this absence heightens the tension in the scene.

PLATE 32:
DEAD AIM-SOUTHWEST (1969), 34 x 50"
Collection Dr. and Mrs. James Budd

*I tried to create a "you are there" effect in this scene,
bringing the outlaws and their rifles so close
up that they seem to spill right out of the frame.*

PLATE 33:
BRONCO BUSTER (1954), 10 x 12″, pencil drawing
Collection Mary Perillo

*Bronco busting, an everyday event that is anything
but commonplace to a man such as myself.*

PLATE 34:
SOUND OF TEXAS (1964), 18 x 30"
Collection L. Tonnett Byrd.

*The Whiteface, a cross between the Texas longhorn and
the British Hereford, was the Texas rancher's dream bull*

PLATE 35:
COMING HOME (1955), 18 x 36"
Collection Mr. and Mrs. Anthony Mastroberti

*My first Christmas card. Catching his first glimpse of
home after a season in the saddle, the cowboy has to
stop a moment to think about what it all means.*

PLATE 36:
SPOOKED (1977), 24 x 30"
Courtesy Empire Art Gallery, Empire, Colorado

The cowboy is trying to hustle the frightened herd back into place, stemming the stampede before it really gets going.

PLATE 37:
PONY EXPRESS (1968), 30 x 24"
Courtesy Wally Findlay Gallery, New York, New York

The Pony Express rider was a hero on a smaller scale than the chief or the general, but a hero nonetheless.

PLATE 38:
DAY IN THE SADDLE (1973), 30 x 24"
Collection Gus L. Constatinides

The cowboy is caught just as he is about to throw the rope. In a good action painting, the momentum should be strong enough to make the viewer believe that he is seeing the frozen act carried through to completion.

PLATE 39:
BRONCO (1970), 18 x 24″
Collection John and Priscilla UpJohn
Difficult as it was to catch these wild horses,
it was easy compared to taming them.

PLATE 40:
BREAKING APACHE (1965), 24 x 34"
Collection Mr. and Mrs. Dwight E. Sarber

Bronco busting, Indian style.

PLATE 41:
SPORTING CHANCE (1958), 26 x 38"
Courtesy Meinhard Galleries, Houston, Texas

*The title is ironic; the buffalo never
had a chance against the Iron Horse.*

PLATE 42:
THE SHERIFF (1959), 24 x 18"
Collection Michael Vergona

One of my few paintings of an old Western town;
I'm more at home on the range.

PLATE 43:
THE RENEGADES (1967), 24 x 30''
Courtesy Images Gallery, Minneapolis, Minnesota

There was no law that said only white men could be outlaws.

PLATE 44:
HORSE THIEF (1980), 50 x 38''
Courtesy Funk and Wagnalls Collection

The axis of mounted and riderless horses moving from right to left across the canvas gives the viewer a real sense of swift movement.

BLACKFEET WARRIOR

3

The Indians and Their Land

THE UNITED STATES is built upon a foundation of Indian graves, of that there is no doubt. When Europeans first came here there were more than forty million Indians already living in the Americas. At the beginning of this century that number had dwindled to about two hundred thousand. Now there are about a million and a half native Americans living throughout the country.

Disease—even the common cold—was a great factor in wiping out the Indian population. Whole tribes were decimated because they had no natural immunity to the sicknesses the whites brought to this continent. Of course there was the factor of greed as well. Land that had been lived on by the Indians for thousands of years was grabbed by whites who justified their action, at first, in the name of Christendom, and later in the name of the government.

In three of my major paintings I have tried to depict the wilds of North America before the advent of the Europeans. One is *The First Explorer.* This painting shows a solitary Indian paddling a canoe through a marshy area. It is one of the very few scenes I've done that is set in the East. The shore toward which the brave is traveling is done in a very impressionistic manner. The misty distance conveys a sense of marvel and implies the difference in the way the Indians perceived time. For them, time was not a straight line with the past behind and the future in front. Time moved in a circle or a spiral. If a man dreamed something and it came true, then it had happened twice and the

Plate 46

man experienced the same thing twice, once in spirit-time, so to speak, and once in awakening time. The Indian depicted in *The First Explorer* may have believed that it was his medicine (the power which guides destiny) to be an explorer. So he approached each new shore not as a mere destination, but with both a sense of awe and a preparedness to see something that his dreams had already revealed to him. This is the kind of perception of the world that allows for a mythology. There was an abundance of mythology in Indian life and each brave viewed his life as sort of a part of a vast epic poem which would be told around council fires throughout the ages.

Cliff Dwellers is another painting that deals with the theme of the Indians before the white men came. There is an idyllic quality here. The young man is courting the girl sitting barebreasted on the wall. Her mother looks on from the cool shade of her cliffside home. The girl's younger brother is obviously unconcerned with the romantic goings on.

Plate 45

The Indians of Colorado and New Mexico who were cliff dwellers were farmers. The verdant valley beside the river indicates cultivation of the land.

I had a lot of fun painting this particular piece. It felt, as I worked, as if I were constructing the home stone by stone. The logs jutting from the walls were beams for support. In my travels throughout the Southwest I have spent a lot of time living with the Indians and poking around in the hills to find scenes that inspired me. When I came upon my first cliff dwelling I knew

PLATE 45:
CLIFF DWELLERS (1979), 26 x 36″
Collection Gus L. Constatinides

Indian cliff dwellings were almost impregnable
fortresses. The setting is Colorado's Mesa Verde.

PLATE 46:
THE FIRST EXPLORER (1975), 30 x 50″
Prudential Collection

Before the white man, the mistiness of the forest represented magical thought patterns of prehistoric people who did not measure time in a limited fashion.

that I would have to do a major painting using this mode of abode as the theme. No one knows what it was that killed off the cliff-dwelling Indians of southern Colorado, whether it was disease or war or famine. But there are none of these people left.

Dead Aim, which shows an Indian warrior full face taking aim with bow and arrow is also set in a time before the white man. You can tell that this painting is before the white man by examining the warrior's clothing—there is no beadwork on his buckskins. The leather band around his wrist is dark and devoid of color. One thing the whites brought with them that the Indians found useful was glass beads. The story of how the island of Manhattan was purchased for twenty-six dollars' worth of trinkets is by now well known. In truth, though, beads and trinkets were among the few things, along with rifles and horses, that the Indians found of value among the many "innovations" of the whites.

Plate 47

The most worthless thing given the Indians were promises. This is the story behind *White Man's Promises*. The painting shows a Cheyenne mother kneeling on the land to which she and the rest of her tribe have been moved by the whites. Having fallen to her knees in passion and anger, the woman announces to her sons, "These are the promises of the white man." She grabs a handful of sand and lets it drift through her fingers. "The white man's promises are as worthless as this land they have given us. No food will grow in such barren soil. And at the first shift of the winds the grains of sand are blown away. These are the promises of the white man."

Plate 48

PLATE 47:
DEAD AIM (1969), 18 x 24"
Prudential Collection

*Sighting the enemy, the intense concentration of this Cheyenne warrior
is portrayed in his face and in the tensed muscles of his arm.*

PLATE 48:
WHITE MAN'S PROMISES (1972), 24 x 32"
Collection Richard Habeeb

To the Indians, the white man's promises were as barren as the sand of the desert land they were given after being driven from their native terrain.

The empty bowl and basket signify the predicament facing this tribe. Starvation is not far off. Over the shoulder of the mother a rack for drying buffalo hides can be seen. It is empty. There are no buffalo left on this new land. The one son holding the knife is ready, even with such meager armament, to avenge his people who have already died at the hands of the white men. The other son stares off into the distance, remembering the green and plenty of the land which was once theirs. It is a somber scene of a people from whom every means of staying alive has been taken. Now all they can rely on is the wormy food provided by the U.S. government.

The Last Sunset shows an Indian warrior lying half-propped against a rock. He is dying, and with the last of his strength he has broken his lance, which lies across his leg. He knows it is useless against the bullets of the whites.

Plate 49

Duck Hunters portrays a happier time. It shows some Sioux hunters heading back from a successful expedition. I have spent considerable time living with the Northern Sioux and Cheyenne on their reservations. They are a very noble people and I have the greatest respect for them. In this painting the Indians are enjoying the springtime. It is still too cold for the cavalry troops to venture into their land and they have decided to go out and get some ducks. The Indians, for the most part, desired a just peace with the white man. They believed that the earth could support both themselves and the whites. Problems arose when the white settlers and their government constantly wanted more. Everywhere the Indian went, the whites followed and killed to get more land. *The Last Frontier* is symbolic of the Indian being driven farther and farther away. The Sioux brave in this painting stares out across the prairie and knows that soon the white man will come here also. He meditates upon the serenity of the earth and wonders if he will ever see a time of peace. He wonders why the Great Spirit has let the white man defeat the Indians.

Plate 58

Of course the Indians never got a just peace. Peace was achieved only when they gave up everything that was sacred to them, even their freedom to roam. While the water flowing in *Duck Hunters* may be washing away the stink of the white man that has come to the earth and innundates even the very soles of the Indians' moccasins, it only half cleanses the hunters. For in their arms they cradle carbines which will soon be making the transition from the peaceful business of providing food to the warfare that was inevitable. The warrior in *The Last Sunset* is a victim of this warfare; the Sioux in *The Last Frontier* will soon become a victim of it. And the Cheyenne in *White Man's Promises* are victims of the "peace" which was finally forced upon them by the sheer number of whites who invaded the country that belonged to the Indians.

Plate 57

Silence is an appropriate statement on the Indian and the westward push of the telegraph. The Indian chopping at the telegraph wires is attempting to silence communication between the white men, and to remove this intrusion into the quietude

Plate 50

PLATE 49:
DUCK HUNTERS (1972), 18 x 24"
Prudential Collection

*The Indians found that the white man's weapons
could be useful for purposes other than war.*

of the vast plains. This communication had the gravest consequences for the Indians, for it was the telegraph that carried the messages from the East which were orders for genocide.

America has much to be proud of today. We can put men in outer space and we can circle the globe in a matter of hours by jet. But our history must not be forgotten, if for no other reason than to serve as an incentive to find ways that are peaceful to achieve what we want.

The Indians were more than symbols or myths. They were a real people, human beings, who had their own mythologies and symbolism. They had families, buffalo to provide them with food and shelter, and a great land. Now we have that same land and the Indians are left with almost nothing.

PLATE 50:
SILENCE (1966), 24 x 18″
Prudential Collection

To the Indians the telegraph was a deadly weapon; it carried
messages of genocide from Washington. The lonely
vastness of the Plains emphasizes the futility of the Indian's gesture.

PLATE 51:
ARAPAHO PARTY (1972), 24 x 30"
Collection M. Laurito

The Arapaho were aligned with the Sioux
and Cheyenne in the Battle of Greasy Grass.

PLATE 52:
PEACE (1970), 6 x 7'; four-panel screen, oil on wood
Collection John and Priscilla UpJohn

One of my largest works, it carries a message
which I believe in fervently—the need for peace.

PLATE 53:
BLACKFOOT HUNTER (1967), 31 x 42″
Collection Dr. and Mrs. Frank Arista

*Winter is the best time for hunting the cougar.
The hunter and his Appaloosa can follow
the big cat's tracks through the snow.*

PLATE 54:
WINTER WARRIOR (1978), 35 x 43″
Collection Robert and James McGinn

*I love to paint the West's magnificent landscapes for their own sake,
but it is always the human presence—awed or contemplative—
which ultimately gives them meaning.*

PLATE 55:
THE BIG SLEEP (1968), 25 x 31"
Collection Arthur Gladstone

The title is meant to be ironic rather than melodramatic.
The Blackfoot returning to camp is very much alive;
he just fell asleep because he was bored to death.

PLATE 56:
DAWN (1980), 38 x 50"
Collection Judy S. Nadel

*This might be the most beautiful moment of the day
in the West. The stillness is overwhelming.*

PLATE 57:
THE LAST SUNSET (1980), 36 x 72"
Collection Mr. Frank S. Nizarre

*Realistic and symbolic at the same time, the dying Sioux represents
his tribe's hopes that died in the years after the Battle of the Little Bighorn.*

104

PLATE 58:
THE LAST FRONTIER (1980), 28 x 50″
Courtesy Warwick Gallery of Fine Art, Ridgewood, New Jersey

*A Cheyenne takes a last look at his beloved landscape
before it is changed by the white man.*

PLATE 59:
BROKEN SILENCE (1978), 32 x 45″
Collection Gus L. Constatinides

*In the stillness of the mountain landscape it is easy
to sense an intruder. Is it animal or human, friend or enemy?*

BUFFALO MAN
(SIOUX)

4

The Buffalo Hunt

AMONG THE PLAINS TRIBES the buffalo was a source of food, clothing, and even shelter, since the tepees of the Sioux, Cheyenne, et al., were made from the hides of the bison (which happens to be the real name for what is often mistakenly called the buffalo). The theme of the buffalo hunt, the young hunters and their ponies pitted against the thundering herds with only lances, or bows and arrows, to bring down these massive beasts, has long been a favorite of mine. I have used it in my sculpture, to create a bronze, as well as in numerous paintings and drawings. And I shall probably continue to use it as long as I paint.

All of my depictions of the buffalo hunt have one thing in common: they all represent the Indian after the arrival of the *conquistadores* from Spain. One can tell this because the works all show the hunters on horseback. It wasn't until the Spanish brought horses, and they escaped and bred, that the Indians captured and made use of mustangs. Before the horses were available the braves used quite primitive means to slay the behemoth.

There is one thing that is true about buffalos—they are some of the dumbest creatures on God's earth. Before the invention of the bow and arrow for use in hunting and warfare, the Indians used clubs to kill the beasts. They would stampede a herd of buffalo over the edge of a cliff by whooping and waving blankets, then go down to the bottom of the cliff and bash in the skulls of any bison left living. These animals are so dumb that they will follow, when scared, any other member of the herd that takes the lead. So in essence all the braves had to do was frighten one into heading for the cliff, keep whooping and hollering, and watch a whole season's supply of meat go head over hooves to its collective death. Not exactly a very romantic picture of the Indian-as-hunter, which is why I have never used it as the theme for a painting or other work. Archeologists know that this was the means for carrying out the hunt because they have found piles of bones at the bases of cliffs and plateaus.

Once the tribes acquired ponies and mastered the art of riding things changed considerably, of course. No longer was it necessary to slaughter the beasts in such a fashion. In the painting *The Hunters and The Hunted* I explore the theme of the buffalo hunt in the manner which is classic among Western painters. That is to say, from the outside of the herd, giving a panoramic view.

In this painting the herd of bison has dwindled due to the westward push of the white man and the wanton slaughter of the beasts for their hides.

The brave is drawing the bowstring taut, his horse is low to the ground in a gallop that is almost out of control as its rider kicks his heels into the pony's belly again, driving it closer to the buffalo. One shot will have to pierce the heart of the charging bison. If that does not fell the creature, the hunter will be forced to share the glory of the kill with his fellow tribesmen who are coming up behind with lances. This sort of teamwork is similar

PLATE 60:
FACE TO FACE (1975), 24 x 30"
Collection David Alexson

This buffalo's mistake was in straying away from his herd.

PLATE 61:
THE LAST HUNT (1979), 54 x 72"
Prudential Collection

A unique and compelling view from inside the hunt.

to that used in the bullfights, except of course there is no cheering crowd. There is only the glow of success that overcomes the successful hunter, and the glory that is his as the story of the hunt is recounted around the campfire when the hunters return to camp with meat.

I put a lot of detail into this painting. Hunting the buffalo was no easy feat. Though the plains were grasslands, they were not smooth and easy riding, as the rises and falls depicted in this picture show. The riders were forced not only to take into account the speed of the buffalo, the fear of their mounts, but also the lay of the land. A wrong move and the horse could topple over, tripped up by the earth, and the rider would tumble into the path of the sharp hooves of his prey.

Plate 62

The painting *Impact* is a rather important painting for me personally. One day my family—Mary, my wife; Annette, my daughter; and my son Stephen—and I were all sitting around the swimming pool. My son was running and throwing himself off the diving board, arms and legs flailing, into the water. I had been thinking all day about finding a new theme for a painting of a buffalo. Suddenly it came to me in a flash—the buffalo charging and picking up the pony with its horns, the rider thrown high into the air by the impact. Stephen's posture as he went off the board would serve as the pose for the Indian rider. I quickly picked up my sketch pad and asked Stephen to do his dive again exactly the same way. He did it but I did not have enough time to capture the action of the pose on paper. I asked

my son to do it again. He did. Still I missed the essence of the
action that I was striving for. I asked him to do it again. And
again. Finally Mary got up and went into the house. She came
out a few minutes and a couple of dives later.

As Stephen took his next leap into the pool, and by this time,
I should mention, he was puffing and sputtering out of breath, I
yelled, "Spread your arms out, spread your arms out!" Mary
snapped a picture with the Polaroid camera she had brought out
while I tried to sketch the movement. I had not even seen her
camera. She told the boy that that was enough and handed me a
snapshot. "No need to drown your son," she said. The painting
Impact turned out quite well and is an unusual treatment of the
buffalo hunt theme.

Another unusual treatment of the buffalo hunt is *The Last
Hunt.* No other Western painter has ever brought the viewer
inside the hunt. The rider on the white horse is clearly the
center of attention. His pose is that of a classical hero. I
purposely exaggerated his musculature in order to bring out his
heroic stature. The buffalos, filling the foreground, take on a
new dimension, larger than life.

I have done numerous studies of the buffalo up close. They
are fascinating to watch and to draw. The movements of their
heads, which have developed instinctively over thousands of
years, are particularly interesting to watch: they shake their

Plate 61

woolly heads up and down and from side to side whenever they are disturbed, before even attempting to move. This is because the main threat to the survival of the buffalo, which dates back to the days when they were so numerous that the few Indians who hunted them were negligible in the development of instincts, was snow. Snow would drive these animals together to stay warm during the blizzards which are so common on the Great Plains. After the storm had passed, the herd would often find itself trapped by the voluminous drifts and depth of the wintry powder. The bulls, who were on the outside of the huddle during the storm, would begin to move their heads back and forth and up and down to shovel the snow away. This natural plowing movement also helped them to find food for grazing when the earth was covered with winter's white coat.

During the summers of 1960 and 1961 I spent a lot of time painting the bison herds that graze along the Mission River in the National Bison Refuge near Moiese. One bull that I got close to still sticks in my mind. He was Gargantuan in proportion and his huge head was dark with a mixture of purple, black, crimson and blue. His hide was a dark brown with tints of orange and yellow. I did some quick sketches of him while he observed me, his nostrils distending, growing larger, it seemed, with each breath that he took. I sensed that I was annoying him, that just my presence annoyed him. Mary was watching me from the car

PLATE 63:
THUNDERING HERD (1970), 24 x 30"
Collection B. Giardina

*This is probably the most dangerous way to hunt
the buffalo. The young hunter is proving his bravery.*

PLATE 64:
**THE HUNTERS AND
THE HUNTED** (1959), 24 x 30″
Prudential Collection

*A panoramic treatment
of the theme in which I try to
convey the danger of the hunt.*

and she must have sensed it as well, because she called out that she was afraid and asked me to come back to the car and get away from the beast. But I kept on drawing him. He turned to face me. It was a magnificent frontal view of him and I immediately started another sketch, while he started alternately to paw and pound the earth with his front hooves. Saliva began dripping from his nose and mouth as his breathing became more rapid, his snorts more fierce. I decided that this was one sketch I would have to do from memory. The flapping of the sketchbook as I closed it must have incited him. He charged. I dropped the pencil and pad and ran like a bandit for the car. Mary had the door open and was shouting, "Shoo, shoo, go away," as though that would deter the behemoth. I got into the car just in the nick of time. The bison circled us a few times, then headed back to his herd. It was magnificent to watch him as he pushed at the herd and then hustled the laggers into formation. He was in charge and he drove them across the Mission River. As I went out and picked up my pad, he stopped for an instant and looked back, as though daring me to follow. Then he charged round the herd and led them off.

All this time spent observing the bison in their natural habitat contributed to the strength of *The Last Hunt.* The wildness of their eyes and saliva spewing from their mouths gives life and action to the scene. The rider in their midst is more than an ordinary hunter. I conceived him as a classical, tragic hero and the hunt itself as a kind of "twilight of the gods,"

PLATE 65:
BUFFALO HUNT (1977), 24 x 30"
Collection Louis DeSantis

Another version of the traditional Western theme.

foreshadowing the destruction of the great herds of buffalo and, thus, of the Indian way of life.

The same idea is treated in a much lighter vein in *Sporting Chance*, which depicts a herd of buffalo halting a train. The title is ironic; the buffalo never had a chance after the steam-powered trains began their movement westward. Hunters like Buffalo Bill Cody slaughtered the beasts by the thousands to supply meat for the labor gangs who laid the tracks across the continent. Once the trains were able to traverse the country, the wanton killing increased: it was easier to transport the hides of the animals back east by rail. The use of the small herd dramatizes this and, I think, makes the title particularly apt.

Plate 41

Were it not for the efforts of conservationists, particularly the great president Theodore Roosevelt, these critters would now be extinct. I am grateful that the efforts of these farseeing people saved the species. Without the protection afforded the North American bison, many of my paintings would probably not exist; nor would one of the most magnificent creatures that still runs wild.

PLATE 66:
CLOSING IN (1976), 30 x 24″
Courtesy Images Gallery, Minneapolis, Minnesota

As in my other treatments of the buffalo hunt, excepting The Last Hunt, *this painting portrays the theme in a manner typical of the Western genre.*

PERILLO © '80

CHEYENNE

5

The Bronzes

ABOUT 1960 THERE WAS an Indian show called "Indian Culture" which toured the Tri-State area. I was invited to take part, which I did, sitting in a display booth, with my paintings around me, sketching. One afternoon a woman asked me what tribe I was from. I folded my arms across my chest in mock-Indian fashion and said, "Neapolitan Tribe." Her expression was something to see. The Indians with whom I was sharing the booth got quite a laugh out of the incident.

It was at this same show that I first met Chief John Big Tree, one of the three chiefs who modeled for the back of the Buffalo head nickel. He was also the model for what is probably the most famous sculpture of the American West—James Fraser's *The End of The Trail.*

I asked the chief what it had been like to pose for Fraser. He told me that the great master used to make him sit on a carpenter's sawhorse. The more tired and depressed he got, the more Fraser would become inspired. The sculpture dramatizes the dejection of the American Indian at the loss of his native land, and over the years it has come to symbolize the final defeat of the Indians by the white man. He said he had mixed feelings about modeling. The money was good and he admitted that he liked the attention.

I asked him if I could do a sketch of him. He agreed. When I was finished I offered to pay him for his time, but he refused the money, saying that one of the younger Indians at the show had told him about me and that he knew I was a struggling artist.

That was the beginning of a friendship that lasted several

years, until Chief Big Tree's death. He often visited Mary and me at our Staten Island home. Whenever he came, Mary would make a big fuss over him and cook a big meal. John loved Italian food almost as much as he loved to talk.

He was a great raconteur. He loved to talk about his days as a movie star—he had played in *Drums Along the Mohawk* with Henry Fonda and Claudette Colbert, and in several films with John Wayne. John Big Tree, after a couple of glasses of wine, would proclaim that he was by far a better actor than Wayne and felt that he should have received top billing. I would respond that his English was worse than an Italian immigrant's. This would set him off speaking his native Seneca. He would jabber away at Mary and me. Neither of us understood a word he was saying, of course. Eventually I would start responding in Italian. Before long Mary would be in stitches laughing. Then I would break up myself. John, however, would maintain an absolutely serious look on his face. It was not that he was angry with us. I know that because I asked him once. It was just that he had been raised to believe that it was unseemly for a chief to laugh.

John Big Tree always used to say to me that when he went to the happy hunting grounds he would be the biggest and best chief there. I'm sure he is. Whenever I think of him, I see him sitting atop a large stallion, pointing down through a blue sky at the earth.

Several years after John died I found some drawings I had done of him. It was at this same time that I had begun to sculpt and I decided to model some sculpture after the drawings. It

PLATE 67:
BUFFALO HUNT (1970), Height 17", Base 19" wide, Bronze
Prudential Collection

*An action piece that is meant to convey the masterful
horsemanship of all the Plains tribes.*

PLATE 68:
BUFFALO (1970), Height 11″, Bronze
Collection Manford Peare

This is a detail from my larger sculpture Buffalo Hunt.

seemed very appropriate considering John's long involvement with Western sculpture.

John Big Tree and I had often talked about Chief Black Kettle of the Southern Cheyenne nation and I figured that would be a good place to start. My bust of *Chief Black Kettle* was modeled after the sketches of John Big Tree.

Plate 69

In the history of the American West no one figure has been ignored as much as the great Chief Black Kettle. Little has been written about him. Perhaps this is because his story represents one of the blackest marks in the bloody chronicle of the policy of genocide that was carried out by the government of this country against the native Americans.

Black Kettle was the "top" chief of the Southern Cheyenne tribe in the year 1864. He was in the process of trying to negotiate a treaty of peace with the white men of the Colorado Territory. His efforts led to the massacre of most of his band, and that of several other Cheyenne chiefs.

The reasons behind this war tell the story of the greed of the white man, and the absolute dishonesty displayed in almost all dealings with the Indians. In 1860, several chiefs for the Arapaho and the Cheyenne signed a treaty which cancelled out the treaty of the Arkansas of 1850. Black Kettle refused to sign because he saw that his tribe would be getting a bad deal: the white man wanted to limit his tribe to living on a small parcel of arid land in eastern Colorado. Previously the Cheyenne and Arapahos had a vast reserve on which they hunted and led a peaceful existence.

PLATE 69:
CHIEF BLACK KETTLE (1970), Height 19½″, Bronze
Prudential Collection
*A portrait of the leader of the Southern Cheyenne
based on sketches of Chief John Big Tree.*

The white men considered the treaty in effect even though
Black Kettle refused to sign it.

Soon after the signing of the treaty an Osage Indian, in the
employ of the cavalry as a scout and guard, shot and killed a
Cheyenne who was drunk on whiskey, but unarmed. At this
time there was friction between the chiefs and the Dog Soldiers,
a group of young Cheyennes, who acted as a kind of "police"
force. They did not follow the chiefs because they believed that
peace was impossible with the white man. These Dog Soldiers
went on the warpath after the killing of the drunken brave.
Hostilities increased and soon all the Cheyenne were considered
enemies by the settlers in Colorado and the more citified folks
who ran the territorial government from Denver.

In August of 1864 George Bent, a mountain man and trader
who was known as "Little White Man" among the Cheyenne,
drafted a letter to the commander of Fort Lyon requesting a
peace council. The letter was signed by Black Kettle and various
other minor and sub-chiefs. In November, Black Kettle and
Chief White Antelope led their people to the fort. The
commander was one Major S. J. Anthony of the First Colorado
Cavalry.

Major Anthony assured the Cheyenne that they could camp
along the banks of the Sand Creek in safety. He asked for their
weapons and the Cheyenne surrendered everything but a few
bows and arrows for hunting.

At the same time Colonel Chivington, a former preacher
who decided that Indians made better corpses than they did

Christians, was leading the Colorado Third Cavalry (known then as the "bloodless Third" because they had yet to engage in battle with the Indians) toward Sand Creek and Fort Lyon. With Chivington were the C, E and F companies of the First Colorado Cavalry, in addition to the Third. In all, there were about seven hundred troops, a small army really. With them they had four twelve-pound mountain howitzers.

When this mounted force reached Fort Lyon Major Anthony and his troops joined them, and they headed out on the night of November 28 for Sand Creek.

Black Kettle and White Antelope had an encampment of about six score tepees, on a bend in the almost dry river.

The cavalry surrounded the camp and at dawn they attacked. Black Kettle could not believe it was happening. He took an American flag given him by a previous, friendly commander of Fort Lyon and hoisted it above his lodge, with a white flag of truce below the stars and stripes. He was sure this would stop the charge because he figured that the troops had made a mistake. But it was a useless effort. White Antelope, in the meantime, went and stood in the middle of Sand Creek with his arms folded across his chest to signify that he and his people were unarmed. He was cut down by a hail of bullets.

The people of the tribes, of course, fled in panic. About eighty women and children and some old braves and very young men dug holes into the banks of Sand Creek in an effort to hide. They were discovered and every one of them was murdered. Afterwards the cavalry troops went about through the bodies and scalped all the dead and cut off any ears or fingers which were adorned with jewelry.

All told, between four and five hundred Indians were slaughtered that day. Black Kettle was reported slain, but this was not the case. Several years later, at the signing of yet another treaty, he appeared and proclaimed his shame at having allowed his people to be misled and butchered. Even so, he signed this last treaty as a representative of his tribe.

There was an investigation of the Sand Creek Massacre in Denver, and the only officer who had not allowed his men to fire on the Indians testified against Chivington and the others. This officer was assassinated during the investigation, on his wedding night.

On November 27, 1868, almost four years to the day after the Sand Creek Massacre, General George Armstrong Custer led the Seventh Cavalry in a sneak attack on a sleeping village of Cheyenne. The Indians were encamped along the Washita River. Again it was dawn, and again the leader of the band was Black Kettle. Custer led his troops into the village and they slaughtered almost every one of the Indians, including Black Kettle.

In my bust of *Chief Black Kettle* it is the cohesion of disparate elements that contributes to the strength and uniqueness of the piece. The long eagle feather coming from the back of the head to the left shoulder accentuates the asymmetrical placement of the hair ornaments. At the same time, this eagle feather intersects with the jutting buffalo bone knotted atop the head.

These angles of the feather and the buffalo bone create a visual geometric balance; they work together to accent the upward thrust of the strong, noble chin. The baubles and beads in the foremost braid, as well as the cylindrical ornament resting on the breastbone, break up the overwhelming massiveness the metal would otherwise lend to the piece. These minutiae also add liveliness to the visage by reflecting in miniature, especially the beads, the contours of the cheeks and lips.

The flood of hair to the right shoulder, and the looping sweep of the braids on the left offset the powerful column of the neck, which leads the viewer's attention to the center of the face. The eyes, which peer back when the bust is viewed at eye level, animate the face. As with any successful sculpture, this bust of *Chief Black Kettle* must be viewed in the round to be truly appreciated.

When I finished *Chief Black Kettle* I had a sense of having really joined the tradition of Western artists. Having had the honor and inspiration of knowing Chief John Big Tree of the Senecas contributed greatly to this feeling.

Sculpting came quite easily to me. One of my former students, a woman who had not been too successful with painting, came to me one day and showed me some sculpture she had done. Her work was quite good. I immediately wanted to know the mechanics of sculpting. She told me that all I needed was an armature, clay, and the right tools. I was on my way out the door to the art supply store almost before she was finished talking. I started working that same day and immensely enjoyed this new medium—the texture of the clay in my hands, the three-dimensionality that is missing in painting—it was like a revelation to me.

As in the bust of *Chief Black Kettle,* the drawings of Chief John Big Tree served as the model for the brave in my sculpture *Cry of Vengeance.* Sometime before this I had done a painting of the same title *(Cry of Vengeance)* using the same sketches. The same narrative underlies both the painting and the sculpture: a Sioux who was out hunting came back to his camp and found that all the men had gone out after a group of Crow they had spotted. The Sioux and the Crow were the fiercest of enemies. He decided to wait for the rest of the men to return. After a while one of the women began to get worried and she asked this man to go out and look for the others. So the Sioux took off in search of his comrades. It was easy for him to follow their trail, and he rode for a couple of hours in pursuit. His horse began to whinny and snort as he approached a small rise. He rode forward slowly. There, at the top of the rise, he found his friends all slaughtered. In the painting I have the bodies littering the ground around the brave on his pony. By isolating the brave and pony in the sculpture *Cry of Vengeance,* that is, leaving out the bodies, the piece still retains the dramatic qualities of the painting, while the narrative metamorphoses into metaphor. On canvas the brave swears revenge against the Crows who massacred his tribesmen. In bronze the upraised lance and face staring to the heavens become the expression of a man raging against injustice. Here the fists clenched around both the reins

Plate 71

PLATE 71:
CRY OF VENGEANCE (1970), Height 22″, Bronze
Collection Manford Peare

A sculpted version of a theme treated in the 1961 painting.

and the lance, together with the arched, tensed torso of the brave atop the horse, work to signify the anguish and anger of all Indians when confronted with the history of their treatment on this, their own, continent. Placing the pony and rider on a piece of ground rising towards the front of the sculpture, while remaining true to the original narrative of the painting, also allowed me to add to the sense of dejection and sorrow mingling with anger, through the downward positioning of the horse's head.

Cry of Vengeance was cast, as were all my other bronzes, in an edition of twelve with three artist's copies. It quickly became the most popular of my sculptures and sold out almost immediately.

In contrast to the meditative nature of *Cry of Vengeance*, my *Buffalo Hunt* bronze is pure action, from the flying braids of the hunter, to the sad yet expressive face of the buffalo crumpling in pain and death. This Indian exemplifies the great horsemanship of all the Plains tribes. Note how the rider holds in his teeth the rope that guides the horse. Lacking the accoutrements of saddle and stirrups, he maintains his balance by jockeying side to side in a rocking fashion that matches in rhythm the wild flailing gallop of the pony. The deftness and sureness of the hunter is unmistakable: only seconds after the first arrow has entered the buffalo's body, another missile is already notched and ready to fly.

Plate 67

The buffalo, which was taken as a detail and cast as *Buffalo*, a separate sculpture, is a tribute to the magnificent power of these creatures. Even with an arrow piercing its heart the beast refuses

Plate 68

to die. The muscles of the neck are rippled and bunched in the effort of arching and twisting its massive, humped back as it attempts to throw off the pain with sheer brute force. The buffalo's pronounced rib cage, juxtaposed against the steeled muscles of the horse responding to the Indian driving it closer to the kill, emphasizes its vulnerability and the weakness and imminent death. This central detail drives home the fact that it is the Indian, the hunter, who is master of the situation.

Plate 70

My bronze of *Sitting Bull* shows the mighty chief in action. His mouth is open as he shouts his war cry, shouts the questions, "What have you done to my people, my land, my culture? Why did you destroy the Indian?" The lance points directly at the viewer; he is demanding as much as questioning. The rearing horse gives the sense of Sitting Bull having stopped only for a moment to question, for he was a man with a mission—he must ride onward, must unite the various tribes of the Plains and drive the white man from the Indian lands. Like Napoleon, Sitting Bull had a vision and he acted upon it. This bronze is successful in portraying the power and spirit of the great leader.

All my bronzes were cast at the Roman Bronze Works in Corona, Queens, New York.* This is where Remington, Russell, Baldwin, Proctor, all the greats of Western art, did their casting. I feel honored to be part of that tradition. However, because of the ease with which sculpting came to me, I could never make it my life's work. Painting is the real challenge and the real love of my life.

---

* Philip Schiavo, the present owner—his family founded the Roman Bronze Works—says, "In my grandfather's time it was Remington; in my time it's Perillo."

—*co-author.*

PERILLO
© 80

SIOUX BRAVE

6

The
Mighty
Chiefs

IT WAS MY FATHER who first inspired me to draw, though somewhat inadvertently. He was an immigrant, from Naples, Italy, and at night he attended history classes at a nearby school. He wanted to learn everything he could about this vast, great nation he had come to call home.

I can recall one night, when I was about six years old, my father was retelling what he had learned that evening in school. We were sitting in the kitchen and the aroma of my mother's cooking was still fresh in the air. Papa was relating the tale of Chief Tecumseh and how he had helped the Americans during the War of 1812.

I was so excited by this story that I went to my room and sketched out the whole thing in pencil before going to sleep that night.

The next morning I awoke early enough to run downstairs before my father left for work. He was very impressed, amazed really, at seeing my drawing. He promised me another story when he got home.

That began what could almost be called a tradition in our house. My father always seemed to have a great story about some Indian or another. The tales he told of their bravery were fantastic. I would draw my impressions of these sagas and my father and mother were always delighted with the results.

It wasn't until about three years later, when I started going to the library to read the stories my father had told me, that I realized he had made many of them up—the names, the places, everything. When I asked him about this, why he had done it, he replied, "To keep you drawing, Gregory. You are very good at it."

For me this mix of fact and fantasy became my life's work. In a narrative painting or sculpture like *Cry of Vengeance* I begin to fantasize the whole story until I can visualize in my head that moment I want to capture on canvas or in clay. And in painting the great chiefs I of course had to fantasize a bit because the chiefs were not available to me as models. In some cases I worked loosely from existing photographs. Other times I had to imagine what the great chief might have looked like, and choose a model who corresponded to my idea.

Plate 85
Plate 71

One thing is consistent in all my treatments of the leaders of the Indians—I paint them all with majesty. I once made a promise to myself that I would always paint the chiefs of the different nations as noble men, at the height of their glory.

Majesty is very much the theme of my painting *His Kingdom*, though the solitary figure on horseback is not meant to represent any one particular chief. He is a composite of features of all Plains tribes, almost archetypal in his power and pose. His coup stick is wrapped in beaver fur and his headdress contains innumerable eagle feathers. I kept the colors muted, placing the scene in winter, because I wanted to emphasize the respect that the Indian chiefs, even in all their glory, had for nature. Except for the red blanket, which draws attention to the mounted chieftain, he seems almost to blend into his surroundings, so much is he a part of them.

Plate 73

When I paint I draw with the brush, as well as apply color. In *His Kingdom* this technique is especially successful if you examine the rocks and mountains in the panorama. For such a small painting (8 × 24 in.) it has a great sense of depth, created by the different planes stretching into the distance. The brushstrokes effect this depth by multiplying the contours of the mountains behind the rocks, and then by juxtaposing tiny dabs of pine trees. This subdued effect will not always work, but in this painting it is successful.

RED CLOUD *(Oglala Sioux)*

I have done two paintings of Red Cloud, the first of which now hangs in the Crane American Indian Collection in the Denver Museum of Natural History.

In the long and bloody history of the native American versus the white man no one person was more noble and more tragic than Red Cloud. He was a man of peace and a voice of reason amid the senseless killing. Unfortunately, as is so often the case when you study the history of any conflict between two groups of people, there was no room for a reasonable stance in the old West. That is the tragedy of Red Cloud, a tragedy which I also tried to portray when painting this piece.

Plate 72

I used details in the portrait to solidify this feeling of the tragic without becoming overly sentimental. Thus the empty peace pipe is held opposite the beadwork coming over the shoulder—glass beads were unknown to the Indians before the coming of the white man—symbolizing Red Cloud's wishes for peace and harmony once the whites had arrived in his country.

PLATE 72:
RED CLOUD (1963), 27 x 23″
Courtesy Denver Museum of Natural History

*I wanted to convey the image of a man of peace and
a voice of reason amid the senseless killing.*

The detailed plumage of the headdress connotes his great
standing as a chief.

Red Cloud had no hereditary claim to chieftainship. He
became a leader because he had such a forceful personality. By
the time he was in his thirties he had many people following
him. It was in 1865 that the U.S. Government first became aware
of the existence of this great man. The government undertook to
build a road from Fort Laramie, Wyoming to the newly
discovered gold deposits in Montana. Red Cloud was the leader
of the Indians, both Sioux and Cheyenne, who opposed the
building of this road. The presence of a constant stream of
prospectors would destroy what was quickly becoming the last
good hunting grounds. The bison were becoming scarcer and
scarcer.

Red Cloud had the mistaken idea that the whites actually
wanted to have peace with the Indians. He believed that the
white man and the Indian were both watched over by the same
Great Spirit, that there was only a difference in the color of their
skin. Why, Red Cloud wondered, could the Sioux and the
palefaces not share the vast reaches of America? Surely there was
enough land for both.

This judicious attitude was of course not shared by the
whites infected with gold fever and greed. So the government
ordered the road into Montana built. Red Cloud had no choice.
He and his followers seized a camp of surveyors and held them
captive for two weeks. He wanted to make his point to the
government of the whites without bloodshed. But nothing came

PLATE 73:
HIS KINGDOM (1978), 8 x 24"
Collection Joe Auletta

Majesty as embodied in all Plains chieftains.

PLATE 74:
RED CLOUD (1970), 50 x 30″
Prudential Collection
*A tragic figure who had the mistaken idea
that the white man wished for peace with the Indian.*

of this action. Red Cloud had to let the hostages go because some
of the younger men wanted to kill them.

After other attempts to gain fair treatment for his tribe, Red
Cloud was finally driven to take up arms. At the head of a force
of two thousand warriors, he laid seize to Fort Kearney, one of
the garrisons recently built along the new road. It became
impossible for the soldiers to even import enough food for their
horses, unless the wagons carrying supplies were guarded by a
strong force of bluecoats. The soldiers soon began to eat their
horses because Red Cloud and his men made it impossible to
hunt for fresh meat.

In November, 1868, a temporary peace, of sorts, was
established. It seemed to be a total victory for Red Cloud. The
terms of the treaty stipulated that the Sioux would have the
boundaries of whatever land they claimed as their own formally
recognized and honored by the whites. Red Cloud himself
refused even to sign the treaty until all the garrisons had been
withdrawn.

From that day on the chief never took up arms against the
white man. And he had plenty of reason to, of that there can be
no doubt. The treaty was of course broken and the garrisons
were reestablished. Promises of food were made, so that the
Indians would not have to hunt (and therefore not have to carry
weapons). Red Cloud's people almost starved to death on several
occasions because the bandits called government agents sold
elsewhere the food destined for the tribe.

Red Cloud took several trips to Washington to sign treaties

and to plead the case of the Indians. His stance was always respectful, he coined the term "Great Father" in addressing the president. Probably no other Indian tried harder to make the white man understand that the Indians were human, too, with human needs and wants. He needed the belief that he would see that day to continue for so long.

My second painting of *Red Cloud*, which shows him standing in the foreground of a montane landscape, is an unusual one for me in several respects. For one thing, it is a "landscape portrait," and I do not normally place a lone subject, unless on horseback, in a landscape, though I did this with several of the chiefs.

Plate 74

Another unusual aspect of this work is the use of color. This was the first time I had ever used such a bright array of costume. I paid particular attention to the plumage of the headdress once again, just as in my first portrait of *Red Cloud*. However, this time I used almost no white. It is quite fanciful, this headdress, but it was a pleasure to paint.

I played with the shadows of the clouds in this piece, as you can see by the contrast of the two shades of the ground around the chief's feet. Overhead a dark cloud has cast its shadow on Red Cloud, which is an appropriate use of symbolism—the shadow of the cloud representing the coming of the white man. In this particular painting I also used the lay of the land itself as a symbol. From the tops of the mountains to the bottom of the arroyo behind Red Cloud, the land is all converging toward the center of the painting. As a chief, the lands of his ancestors and his tribe were of greatest concern to him.

COCHISE and MANGAS COLORADAS
(Apache)

In my portraits of Cochise and Mangas Coloradas I bring
together two Apache leaders who roamed over the Southwest
and refused to be dominated by the white man. Mangas
Coloradas, with his red headband and stone face, is
quintessentially Apache. There is no pain in his eyes, even
though he lived to see the decimation of his people by the white
man. By using a blue background I was able to draw the viewer's
attention to the powerful face and to the skin tones and bone
structure. The Apache man who sat for this portrait was quite
honored when I told him he was modeling for a portrait of the
chief who was Cochise's greatest ally.

In my "landscape portrait" *Cochise* I portray the great
Apache leader as an aged man—old, but not broken by age—who
is still proud. As in the landscape portrait *Red Cloud* I use the
backdrop of countryside to emphasize that it was his tribal lands
that Cochise waged war to retain.

Cochise fought his first battle at age seventeen, after his
father and many members of his tribe had been tricked and
murdered by Mexicans. For help, he went to Mangas Coloradas
of the Mimbreno Apaches. Mangas Coloradas (which means
"red sleeves", a name the chief was given because of his habit of
wearing red long underwear obtained from the white man—by
what means is uncertain) swore to help Cochise avenge his
father. Together the two chiefs mounted a force of one hundred
men and returned to Concurpe, the scene of the massacre. There

Plate 75
Plate 76

they swept down in the night and killed everyone in the town
except for the children, whom they took with them. Leading
away all the horses, the Apaches returned to what is now called
Arizona.

On the way back they were chased by Mexican soldiers. It
was then that Cochise distinguished himself for the first time as
the great strategist he would come to be known as, a reputation
that would eventually lead Colonel Reuben F. Bernard,
Commander of Fort Bowie, Apache Pass, to say in a military
dispatch to Washington: "Not only is Cochise the most
intelligent hostile Indian on the American continent, but he is
one of the greatest military men of all time. Unfortunately, all
he knows of the white man are their evil deeds."

What Cochise did was this, and it was really quite simple:
using two scouts as decoys, he lay in waiting with Mangas
Coloradas and the other Apaches above a pass. The two scouts
pretended not to see the galloping Mexican troops until they
were almost upon them. Then they rode through the pass with
the Mexicans in hot pursuit. The Apaches let loose volley after
volley of arrows and felled the Mexicans. All but three or four
were killed. And thus did Cochise avenge his father.

The history of Cochise and Mangas Coloradas is a tale of
treachery and vengeance. Mangas Coloradas was taken captive
by the cavalry, tortured and murdered. Cochise was never
captured, and the war he waged cost many hundreds of paleface
lives. At one point he thought he had actually begun to drive the
white man from his homeland. That was during the Civil War,

160

PLATE 76:
MANGAS COLORADAS (1958), 20 x 16″
Prudential Collection

The Apache leader who was called Mangas Coloradas—"red sleeves"—
because he wore the red long underwear of the white man.

when all the soldiers were being recalled to fight in the South.

After the Civil War was over, a man named Thomas Jeffords came to visit with Cochise. He was tall, red-bearded fellow who showed no fear. He was the head of the local Pony Express office and he had come to try and strike an agreement with the Apaches so that his riders could go through their country without being killed.

This man Jeffords went on to become great friends with Cochise, and eventually the two became blood brothers. Eventually, under President Ulysses S. Grant, peace was made with the Apaches. They were given the lands, in a treaty negotiated by General Oliver O. Howard, that now comprise most of Cochise County in Arizona. In June of 1874 Cochise died of some sort of disease. He refused to see a white man's doctor. Four braves, Tesabestinay—Cochise's wife—and Tom Jeffords took the great chief up into the mountains, where he was buried. Jeffords took an oath that he would not reveal the burial place of his old friend and blood brother. And to this day, no one knows where Cochise was buried.

Plate 77

I did another painting, *Cochise Mounted*, which captures the chief at the height of his glory. Using menacing skies, I created the perfect background for a chief who staunchly, yet bloodily, defended his tribal homeland. Once again, as in *Lonesome Cowboy*, the colors on this canvas might be hard for the uneducated eye to believe. Yet, as anyone who has spent time in the Southwest will tell you, they are true to nature. The reflection of the mauve sky on the chief's boots acts to blend the

COCHISE MOUNTED (1966), 36 x 24"
Prudential Collection

The chief at the height of his glory set
against the menacing sky of the Southwest.

figure with his surroundings. He wears no headdress beyond the
bandana, which was typical of the Apaches at this time. The
streaked sky in the middle of the painting creates a break
between the heavy clouds and the plane of the earth. The view
angled upwards towards the chief heightens his majesty. The
play of sunlight and shadow on both the rider and the horse,
combined with the ever-so-slight exaggeration of the color of the
leafy scrub bush beneath the horse add life to the piece.

GERONIMO and VICTORIO *(Apache)*

Plate 78
Plate 79

After the death of Cochise, the leadership of the Apaches fell
upon Victorio and Geronimo. These chiefs fought with great
vigor against both the settlers and the cavalry troops who had
invaded their lands. Victorio eventually took his band to
Mexico where he became a notorious renegade, dauntlessly
refusing to respect the border. He continued to lead his braves
back and forth across the Rio Grande until his death in the late
1890's. I portrayed Victorio with typical Apache features. His
wild hair is symbolic of his refusal to bend to the law of the
whites. His deeply-etched face also shows great determination
and strength. I placed the gold earring in his ear to show the
influence of Mexico upon him, and as a somewhat romantic
flourish.

Geronimo opted to stay in the United States when Victorio
went south. His people were mistreated on the San Carlos

PLATE 78:
VICTORIO (1975), 16 x 20"
Prudential Collection

I portrayed this Apache chief with the Mexican vest he always wore.
He "carried his enemy on his back" to keep his hatred strong.

PLATE 79:
GERONIMO (1979), 30 x 36"
Courtesy of Vague Shadows, Ltd.

*This great Apache leader was one of the most feared Indians
in the history of the conflict with the white man.*

reservation and Geronimo went on the warpath against the
whites. As a warrior he became one of the most feared Indians in
the history of the ongoing conflict between the native
Americans and the white man. In August of 1887, Geronimo
finally surrendered to cavalry troops. He was transported as a
prisoner of war to Florida, then to Alabama, and to Fort Sill,
Oklahoma, where he died in 1909.

CHIEF JOSEPH *(Nez Perces)*

It is doubtful that a more noble or wise man than Chief
Joseph ever led the Nez Perces of Oregon and Idaho. He was a
man who loved peace, yet when it came time to fight, when his
back was against the wall, he proved such an able warrior that his
guerilla warfare tactics are still part of the curriculum at West
Point. In my earlier painting of *Chief Joseph*, executed in 1961,
the robe-like blanket wrapped around his shoulders gives him an
apostolic air. In the background I have placed the Cascade
Mountains, which were part of the hunting grounds of the Nez
Perces. There is a simplicity to this work which is in keeping
with Chief Joseph's life. He often said, after the Nez Perces had
been moved east to Kansas, that all he wanted was the right to
live in the land of his forefathers. He was also a great orator who
visited Washington and New York several times to seek relief for
his tribe.

As a leader he was revered by his people and they followed

Plate 80

PLATE 81:
CHIEF JOSEPH (1980), 50 x 38"
Collection Manford Peare

*My second portrait of Chief Joseph is much more exotic than the first . . .
I really outdid myself in the colors of the chief's garb.*

Plate 81

him, in 1877, across half the continent in a flight from the U.S. cavalry troops that were pursuing him. The journey took two months and earned Joseph the reputation as one of the greatest strategists in the history of American warfare. He was especially noted for his ability to use a small force to create a diversion while he led the rest of his people around the bluecoats who seemingly had him trapped. He used this tactic successfully several times before his final surrender in August of 1887. His most famous statement—"I will fight no more forever"—was uttered at this time and is said to have moved even the soldiers and officers who heard him make the speech.

My second portrait of *Chief Joseph* is much more exotic than the first in its use of color and brushstrokes to create texture. It was completed in 1981 and shows the influence of Tiepolo's murals in the Vatican Museum on my portrait paintings. The umber and white background is a technique which Tiepolo used to great effect, and after viewing the murals I began to incorporate the umber tones in my own work.

I really outdid myself in the colors at the chief's garb. The purple of his jacket lends a royal air to the face that could easily be a nobleman in any culture, of a superior nature. The pink of the feathers at his elbow and waist, and on the beaver-wrapped coup-stick, lend an air of gentlemanliness. It has been said that Chief Joseph, on his visits to New York and Washington, had such a courtly air about him that his bows were the equal of noblemen like Sir Walter Raleigh. There is also a cheeriness lent

PERILLO

*This is a pen and ink drawing of a
saluting warrior on horseback.*

to the work by the use of pink. Chief Joseph, after his surrender,
was always able to meet with the white leaders without showing
any self-pity. Though he was far from happy—he died in 1904,
and the doctor attending him said that the cause was a broken
heart—he never let on to those with whom he dealt in his efforts
to seek justice for the Nez Perces.

The Nez Perces tribe are the people who developed the
Appaloosa breed of horses. Were this their only contribution
they would be remembered. But from that tribe came Chief
Joseph, a great orator, statesman, strategist, leader, and human
being. I hope my painting does him justice.

For many years the great chiefs were portrayed in movies and
the other various media as the "bad guys." When I began to
paint them I strove to do everything in my power to offset these
unjust depictions. The chiefs were anything but bad guys or
outlaws. They were honest, noble men who, like all great
leaders, kept in their hearts a strong concern for their people.
Some of the chiefs, like Red Cloud, were great orators. Others,
like Chief Joseph, were peaceful men who were forced to go to
war, and when they did they proved themselves more than equal
to the military strategists of the government. The great chiefs
were defeated by the sheer numbers of the troops and
armaments that opposed them, not because the white man was
their better. I hope that someday people everywhere will
recognize the greatness of these men and remember them with
the respect that is their due.

THE CHARGE
(SIOUX)

7

The Trail to the Little Big Horn

JUNE 26, 1876, the day of the Battle of the Little Bighorn, or Greasy Grass as the Indians called it, brought together the energies of three men—George Armstrong Custer, Crazy Horse, and Sitting Bull. When William R. Leigh painted this battle he chose to focus on the Indians, with Custer a mere speck atop a hill who was seen through a cloud of dust and gunsmoke. Before dealing with this momentous battle I considered various recourses. It was difficult to decide how to handle such an historic occasion. I chose to do several action paintings and portraitures on this theme which do justice, I think, to the story.

CRAZY HORSE

Most accounts by white men that discuss Crazy Horse say he got his name because a wild mustang had charged through the Indian camp on the day that Crazy Horse was born. This is highly unlikely, as the Indians seldom got their adult names until they had proved their manhood.

The Indians say that Crazy Horse took his name from a vision that he had. In the vision Crazy Horse saw himself on a mount that stayed in one place, yet rippled like the shadow of a tree in the wind. In this vision he was given a stone that was supposed to protect him, and when he awoke from this vivid dream he found a stone that was exactly like the one in the vision. After that he always carried it with him in battle and when hunting. According to legend, whenever Crazy Horse was in danger the stone grew very heavy and protected him with its

PLATE 83:
WAR BONNET (1973) , 24 x 18
Collection Carmen J. Rivello

*He was never photographed,
so I used myself as the model.*

magic. Because of the heaviness of the stone, Crazy Horse was always wearing out ponies, forever having to get a new one. Two of Crazy Horse's cousins—Black Elk and Flying Hawk—talked to white men who wrote down what they said about Crazy Horse and other matters. And both of these accounts state that Crazy Horse was a true loner. He never took part in any of the singing, dancing and tale-telling that went on around the Indians' campfires. Nor did he spend very much time with other Indians, preferring to hang around on the edge of the camp. During periods of famine, he would eat less. And when food was very scarce and the hunts were going poorly, he would fast for days on end.

Flying Hawk said that Crazy Horse once had a younger brother who was his favorite and this brother was killed while on a hunting trip to Utah. Crazy Horse was so angered by the death of his brother that he took his wife and went to Utah, camping outside of the settlement of Mormons who had killed his brother, killing one man every morning and every evening for nine days, in revenge. This was the sort of man Crazy Horse was. He is still spoken of with much respect among the Sioux.

By the time Crazy Horse was nineteen years old he had become a revered war chief among the Sioux. Because of my fascination with this legendary Indian, and because no certain photographs of him exist, in 1973 I allowed myself to indulge a fantasy which I had for some time—I painted *War Bonnet*, in which I portrayed myself as Crazy Horse. I placed a magnificent war bonnet atop the chieftain's head, detailing each and every

Plate 83

PLATE 84:
YELLOW HAIR'S END (1975), 45 x 30"
Collection Barry and Debbie Toombs

I tried to capture what Custer must have felt in those final moments: the madness, the courage, the outrage, the realization that this was the end...

bead. The torso I adorned with wild smears of war paint, just as I did the face and neck. By placing the butt of the rifle on the hip I was able to create an unmistakable triangle, thus drawing attention to the several triangles that are the dominant form upon which the painting is constructed, even down to the pine trees on the horizon. I wanted this form to dominate because it lends stability and majesty to the central figure. *War Bonnet* is a good point at which to begin my narrative of Little Bighorn, for it was Crazy Horse who led the Indians into battle on that day.

BRIGADIER GENERAL GEORGE ARMSTRONG CUSTER

Even without his unearned reputation as an Indian fighter Custer would have a place in the history of this country. That is why I could not, as W.R. Leigh did, relegate the young general to the position of a mere speck on the canvas. Custer was, during the Civil War, the youngest man ever promoted to the rank of general. He was also one of the first aerial observers in the history of warfare, going up in hot air balloons to report on Confederate troop movements.

After the Civil War Custer and his wife went west. There he planned to get himself elected president based upon the numbers of Indians he would kill. He did not succeed in these plans, but he did succeed in cutting a somewhat romantic figure, and he considered himself something of a warrior-poet along the lines of Lord Byron in Greece, though without the sexual

liaisons that were Byron's trademark. Custer was by all accounts faithful to his wife and several volumes of their love letters have been published.

But he did design his own uniform, consisting of a floppy sombrero—which, in my painting *Yellow Hair's End*, I show at his feet, upside down—which he took from a fallen Confederate during the war; his tawny brass-buttoned doublet, which he had tailor-made; buckskins; and the ever-present red scarf. This scarf, he once told reporters after a Civil War battle, he always wore so that it would "stand out like a beacon, so my men could gather round me, and always know where I am." It is just possible that this scarf and this attitude caused his downfall. Is it possible that one of his men, fed up with the general's adventures and knowing that death on the knoll at Little Bighorn was inevitable, took aim at the scarf through the turmoil of dust and powder smoke, and shot down Custer? No one will ever know for sure because there were no white witnesses to the General's death, and the Indian versions tell us only who counted first coup. But why would one of his own men shoot him? For the answer to that we have only to look at his record out West.

In the spring of 1867 Custer set out on an Indian hunting expedition with the Seventh Cavalry. The Seventh, I should note here, was composed of a bunch of ne'er do wells for the most part: assassins, immigrants looking for three squares a day; it was more or less the equivalent of the French Foreign Legion in the first half of this century.

Custer led this ill-trained, mutinous bunch on one of the

Plate 84

most disastrous, both personally and professionally for Custer, campaigns in the annals of the American West. The purpose of the expedition was to seek and find and destroy as many Indians as possible. The tribes which he encountered, mostly by seeing the tail-end of their horses, were the Southern Cheyennes, the Arapahos, Commanches and Kiowas. There was little fighting and much forced marching over the rough terrain of Colorado and Kansas.

One night thirty-five of the troops decided that they had all they wanted of Custer and what they considered his wild goose chase. They deserted and were never apprehended. The next night ten more men deserted. Custer gave orders for these ten to be caught, and he issued an order to "shoot to kill" if necessary to bring back the cowards. Three of them were caught.

Custer's ire was so aroused that he decided to make an example of one of the men and ordered him shot. The troops apparently had no stomach for this summary execution because they only wounded the man and he did not die until the Seventh returned to Fort Riley. Along the way Custer got wind of the fact that all of the enlisted men were planning to desert and steal all the horses to boot. The general ordered his officers to stand guard at night, thus averting this mass mutiny.

Well, the upshot of these actions was that Custer was court-martialled at Fort Leavenworth, Kansas. Custer was found guilty on all counts and specifications, a fact that is often glossed over by his various biographers. The findings of the court were sent on to Washington for review because of Custer's rank.

After the review he was suspended from active duty for a

period of one year. This was considered a very lenient sentence by some. But Custer still had friends among the press, because he always made good copy, and the newspapers for the most part took his side.

In September of 1868 Custer's sentence was suspended and he was allowed to return to duty a few months early, in plenty of time to carry out the massacre of Black Kettle and his people while they were camped along the Washita. Not content with simply butchering the Indians, Custer ordered more than seven hundred Indian ponies slaughtered after this encounter. It is interesting that Custer's reputation as an Indian fighter was based on this attack upon sleeping "savages," and one other large run-in with native Americans—the battle at Little Bighorn.

SITTING BULL

Some historians have put forth the theory that when Custer overtook and massacred Black Kettle and his band on the Washita River, Black Kettle was leading his people to join forces with Sitting Bull. And almost ten years later, a year after the Little Bighorn, Chief Joseph told his captors that he had been leading his tribe to join Sitting Bull in Canada. What was it about this Sioux chief that caused other Indians, some almost two thousand miles away, to follow him and to revere his name? Even today, say the name Sitting Bull almost anywhere in the world and people will know that you are talking about the mighty Indian chief. His name is probably as well known as Napoleon's. Like the French emperor and general, Sitting Bull had a spirit of mythic proportions. It was as if he made every move in his life knowing that his footprints, his exploits, would never be blown away, erased by the wind and forgotten by men; that the fact of his existence would be forever chiseled into the annals of human history. There are just so many great stories about Sitting Bull. He was like an Achilles or Ulysses, an epic hero.

For instance, do you know how Sitting Bull got his name? It came about before he was even born. One day Sitting Bull's father and several other Sioux were out hunting. It was springtime, the snow had melted and all across the plains and throughout the hills the sounds of buffalo could be heard: young and old bulls butting heads in contest over some cows; the rutting and mooing and bellowing of the bison as they coupled. This music of life continuing was a magical gift from the Great Spirit to men.

After a day of hunting, Sitting Bull's father, who was called Jumping Badger, and the other men gathered around the campfire to recount stories from the old days and to tell each other how great they had been in the earlier hunt. Suddenly a strange bellowing was heard close by. Then the earth began to shake. All the men round the fire jumped to their feet.

The largest bull buffalo any of them had ever seen was coming along the path towards the campfire. If a man sat upright on his pony he would have had to look up to see this buffalo's chin. It was more than two and a half horses long and its head was a deep, dark brown, the color of the prairie after a herd of a hundred thousand buffalo had stampeded across it and churned

PLATE 85:
CRY OF VENGEANCE (1961), 30 x 40″
Prudential Collection

*A meditative study on the revenge of a Sioux warrior on
the enemy Crow for the slaughter of his tribesmen.*

the earth with their hooves. But its coat was the white of new snow.

This Gargantuan creature came right into the camp of the Sioux braves. One of the men called out, "It is the sacred spirit of the buffalo!" Everyone except Sitting Bull's father fell to the ground and hid their faces. Jumping Badger stood his ground and looked up into the eyes of the giant beast.

The great buffalo was talking in a strange tongue, saying the same thing over and over, "Sitting Bull, Kicking Bull, White Bull, Slow Bull; Sitting Bull, Kicking Bull, White Bull, Slow Bull."

Now all the Indians there heard the buffalo speak, but only Sitting Bull's father understood the words. The buffalo stopped talking for a moment. Then, in the language of the Sioux, it said, "You, man-who-understands-me, these names are sacred. Use them wisely; bestow them wisely." Then the great beast left the camp, the earth trembling beneath his massive hooves.

After the buffalo was gone the men asked, "Who understands what the buffalo-spirit said?"

"I, Sitting Bull, understood," answered Sitting Bull's father, changing his name on the spot. He then told the braves what other names the buffalo-spirit had given to him. The others clamored for Sitting Bull's father to give the names to them so that they could possess their "medicine", or power. The man now called Sitting Bull said, "No, I understood and the names all belong to me."

The next month a son was born to this man and his wife. Everyone knew that the baby would grow up to be a great chief because nine eagles circled the camp as the baby was being born.

And for the first six months after his birth, whenever the baby began to cry, an eagle would appear in the sky and fly over the camp, swooping low over the tepee of Sitting Bull and his wife. This always stopped the baby's wailing.

The baby boy grew strong and tall. At the age of fourteen his father took him on the warpath against the Crow. The Sioux and the Crow had been deadly enemies for as long as anyone could remember. They hated each other. The boy knew this and he wanted to prove himself against his tribe's enemies. When the war party finally spotted a group of Crow the boy dashed ahead on his pony, yelling, "Hoka hey! It is a good day for dying!"

But this was not the day for the young boy to die. No, he killed and counted coup on eight of the enemy, including the leader of the Crow band, whom the youngest pulled from the back of a pony and killed by driving a knife through his heart. When the chieftain was killed, the rest of the Crow hightailed it out of there.

The other Sioux saw this and they were amazed. Singlehandedly, the young boy had driven off more than thirty enemies. The others in the Sioux war party had to content themselves with counting second and third coup on those slain.

When they arrived back at the main camp the young man's father threw a big party. He gave away many horses in honor of his son. Then he announced to everyone gathered that from this day onward, the boy would be called Sitting Bull.

There are many more stories about Sitting Bull. He became very well known as a singer of songs. He had songs for every occasion: love, war, death, birth, hunting. But his favorite songs were about the birds. Sitting Bull loved birds. There is a story behind this, too.

One day the youth was out hunting by himself. It was a beautiful summer day and the sun was shining and Sitting Bull figured, why not? So he hitched his horse to a tree and took a stroll until he found a big old oak that looked tempting. He lay down in the shade of the tree and took a little nap, the songs of birds lulling him to sleep.

Then, all of a sudden, he sensed that something was wrong and he awakened. There was a terrible smell in his nose and everything was dark. He heard a bird sing out, "Do not move, oh great Sitting Bull. Do not move for there is a bear over you." Sure enough, there was a giant grizzly nuzzling his feet. Sitting Bull was directly under the bear's stomach. The stench was terrible, as anyone who has been close to a grizzly will tell you. The bird sang again, "Oh great Sitting Bull, do not move or the bear will crush you." Sitting Bull lay very still. Suddenly he heard the singing of many birds. The forest was full of them. He heard the grizzly begin to grunt and growl. Soon it was howling with rage. It backed off of Sitting Bull and he could see what was happening—hundreds of birds were attacking the bear, darting at it and pecking the great beast with their beaks. The bear was swatting wildly with its paws, but to no avail. Sitting Bull remained very still and finally the bear, having had enough of the birds, took off running and bellowing through the forest.

Sitting Bull got to his feet and thanked the birds. They all twittered and flew off. Sitting Bull stretched and went back to his pony and rode home. From that day onwards he sang in praise of the birds whenever he could.

Because of this story I have portrayed *Sitting Bull* with a falcon with wings spread in a protective manner behind his head. You will notice the absence of eagle feathers, unusual for a chief. Sitting Bull seldom dressed in full regalia; he was too modest to wear the full number of eagle feathers he would have been entitled to, so he preferred to wear one feather or none at all.

Plate 86

Later in his life Sitting Bull toured Europe and the Eastern United States with *Buffalo Bill's Wild West Show*. Thus there are numerous photographs of him and I was able to paint his likeness with an exactness that was not available to me with some of my other subjects.

Neither the story of how Sitting Bull got his name, nor the tale of the chief's friendship with the birds tells us what it was about the chief that made him such a respected figure among the Indians throughout the West. There are several reasons why this was; for one, in 1868 he negotiated a treaty, using a Jesuit missionary as his emissary, which was, amazingly, to the advantage of the Indian. Word of this went out through all the Plains tribes and this is why some people have ventured the idea that Black Kettle may have been on his way to join Sitting Bull at the time of the massacre along the Washita. His prowess as a hunter also greatly contributed to his reputation.

During the four years of peace that he had negotiated, in addition to leading the hunt, Sitting Bull spent a lot of time politicking among the tribes. He had a plan for uniting all the Indians of the West, with the exception of the Crows and Rees

The existence of photographs taken while the Sioux leader was with Buffalo Bill's Wild West Show enabled me to depict an exact likeness. Beaver fur is wrapped around the braid and the bird is a falcon.

who were now riding as scouts for the cavalry. Once the tribes were united, Sitting Bull's plan called for a great war which would drive the whites once and for all from the Plains and Black Hills and would establish an Indian nation forever. Unfortunately, Chief Red Cloud, who held sway over many Sioux, was the decisive and divisive factor in Sitting Bull's plan. Much as the idea of a separate Indian nation appealed to the chief, Red Cloud had already given his word never to bear arms again, and he kept this promise. Also, by the time Sitting Bull had begun to maneuver, Red Cloud had made a couple of journeys to the East and he was aware that there were simply too many white men for the Indians to drive them out.

In addition to being the chief of the hunt Sitting Bull was of course known as a warrior. Among the Sioux men no pastime was more greatly enjoyed then going out on the warpath against some enemies; and Sitting Bull enjoyed these outings as much as the next man. But of course there were often casualties, which did not bother the men so much as it did the womenfolk. Many families were left without someone to provide the meat for winter because of this sport of war.

In 1872 the government broke the treaty with Sitting Bull by sending in surveyors to build a road and forts throughout the Black Hills. Of course Sitting Bull immediately went on the warpath, stirring up warriors among all the different bands to drive the white men away.

Now by this time Crazy Horse was on the scene, and he was quickly rising to prominence as a war chief. Talk was beginning to circulate among the tribe that he was greater than Sitting Bull,

191

PLATE 87:
MISSING WARRIOR (1975), 24 x 30"
Collection Jane and Robert McGinn

Here the riderless horse is symbolic of a comrade fallen in battle. This ceremony was common to all the Plains tribes.

and that Sitting Bull had lost his nerve. This was because Sitting Bull's mother was constantly begging him not to enter into the fights himself.

One day Sitting Bull and Crazy Horse and a combined force of their warriors ran into a party of cavalry. Crazy Horse immediately charged into the cavalry column and began cutting down the soldiers. Then he wheeled his pony around and returned to where Sitting Bull and the rest were watching.

The soldiers had dismounted in the meantime. Sitting Bull's warriors looked to him to see if he would do anything to match the bravery of the wild Crazy Horse. Now Sitting Bull was anything but a fool. On the one hand he was a natural general, and knew that a general best serves his troops from a vantage point removed from the actual fighting. On the other hand he knew that Crazy Horse would have liked nothing better than to become more powerful by means of showing up the great Sitting Bull. Taking all this into consideration, Sitting Bull decided that it was time to teach the young war chief a lesson.

Sitting Bull himself dismounted and slapped his pony on the rump to send him back to safety. Then Sitting Bull sat right down on the ground with the bullets flying through the air all around him, and he took out his pipe and began to smoke. Then he waved and called out for Crazy Horse to join him. Crazy Horse did as the older chief and he rode right out and sat down beside him. But Crazy Horse, whose medicine, as I already explained, was greatest when he was on horseback, did not like the situation one bit. And he liked it even less when they finished the pipe. Because Sitting Bull, who always kept his ponies well trained, stood up and whistled. His mount responded to the whistle by galloping right out to his master. Then Sitting Bull, the soldiers' bullets still flying all around, mounted up and rode slowly back to the edge of the field.

Crazy Horse was always running his mounts right into the ground and therefore never had the time to train them in the way that Sitting Bull did his. He was stranded there. All he could do was get up and run back on foot to join his followers. In that way Sitting Bull proved that he was the wiser and braver chief. He also put a good damper on any talk of Crazy Horse taking over. The young war chief did not resent the lesson. Instead he became one of Sitting Bull's closest allies and best officers.

The next four years were consumed with the conflict with the white man. The Sioux barely had time to hunt. Sitting Bull knew that they were moving toward a decisive confrontation.

JUNE, 1876

Many stories about Sitting Bull were circulated after the battle at Little Bighorn. Most of them said, in essence, that Sitting Bull was an old scared man and that he hid in the hills "making medicine" during the battle. This is just not a true picture of those events.

It is true that, by the time of the Battle of the Little Bighorn, Sitting Bull was known as a holy man as well as a chief. Sitting

195

Bull had great medicine, of that there can be no doubt. All his life he was able to induce himself into hypnotic trances in which he foresaw the future. But what is not true is that the chief was *only* a medicine leader. Were it not for Sitting Bull the tribes that gathered at the Rosebud River, and then at the Greasy Grass, would never have come together. It takes a great leader, a man with fantastic charisma, to unite a people. There can be no argument that Sitting Bull had the necessary qualities.

While the tribes were gathered at the Rosebud in June of 1876 Sitting Bull prepared to go into one of his trances. He wanted it to be powerful, so he knew that it would be physically demanding, but he was ready to endure whatever it took. The best way, Sitting Bull decided, to induce a good vision was through pain. So what he did was enter a medicine lodge (tepee) and take a very sharp knife. Then he peeled back his skin and removed a bit of flesh. He did this one hundred times. His skin was bathed in blood and it must have been very painful. He passed out and stayed out for over ten hours. Just before he came to, he had a very vivid vision in which many white soldiers attacked his encampment and were defeated.

After he related this vision to all the chiefs who had gathered around the medicine lodge a great clamor ensued. The Indians all believed that Sitting Bull had been granted his vision from the Great Spirit because the loss of blood and flesh symbolized the suffering of the Indians. Everyone in the camp had no doubt that they would be victorious.

Two days later, on June 16, a scout came charging into camp saying that he had spotted a wagon train of soldiers led by "Two

Stars" (General Crook). Sitting Bull, Crazy Horse, and other Sioux and Cheyenne chieftains all mounted their ponies and rode at a gallop to a bluff overlooking the Powder River several miles from their camp. There they saw Crook and his detachment of cavalry making their way toward the Indian encampment. This moment is the subject of my painting *War Party*. To the left of center, wrapped in a purple robe of buckskin, the color signifying both his suffering and his majesty, is Sitting Bull. To his immediate left, with the naked torso and upraised lance, sitting atop the pinto, is Crazy Horse. His head is bent slightly foward as he prepares himself for the battle that is to come. Just past Crazy Horse, with the thunderbird on his shield, is a Blue Cloud (Arapaho) chieftain. The Arapahos and the Cheyenne were at this time aligned with Sitting Bull and the Sioux. The Indian at the very far left with the white shield is a Cheyenne, as is the one posed with the red shield over his shoulder as he sits atop the black stallion. The three Indians to the right of Sitting Bull are all Sioux. When posed next to the tense and fidgety Crazy Horse—his pony seems to be in the act of backing up slightly—the robed figure of Sitting Bull seems even more serene and contemplative.

Plate 89

When painting *War Party* I paid special attention to my color palette, especially when working the open airy spaces. There is a definite haziness that is exactly like the haziness of the air in the beginning of summer. This effect also adds to the sense of stillness as the Indians observe the cavalry troops. It contributes to the overall ominousness which I tried to capture.

The lush greens along the river also add to the summertime

feeling of *War Party*. Yet all of the Indians with the exception of Crazy Horse are garbed as though the air might still have a bit of chill in it, which is the case of the weather in the Dakotas in early to mid-June. I worked out all these details in my mind in advance so that there could be no mistaking the time of year and the scene portrayed: the day that General Crook and his troops were routed by the Indians led into battle by Crazy Horse.

When the Indians returned to camp that night there was dancing and celebration. Crazy Horse and the other chiefs went to Sitting Bull and said, "Your vision has been fulfilled." Sitting Bull announced to the council of chieftains that all honor and glory of that day belonged to Crazy Horse. Sitting Bull's vision had specifically shown the troops coming right to the Indian encampment, and this battle had occurred several miles down the Powder River, away from the camp. Sitting Bull insisted that his vision had yet to be fulfilled.

THE BATTLE of GREASY GRASS

When one takes a good look at the battles that Custer fought during the Civil War, one sees a common factor that might shed a little light on his defeat at Greasy Grass: Custer, all throughout the War between the States, was fighting against former classmates from West Point. All these men were trained by the same teachers to wage war in the same fashion as one another. In fact, a former Confederate officer named Rosser, against whom

Custer led his Michigan Volunteers in the Shenandoah Valley, traveled with Custer out West and they often spent time going over their old campaigns.

What I'm leading up to here is the fact that when George Armstrong Custer fought against military strategists who had the same background and schooling as himself, he did fine. But when he came up against the American Indians, he was at a total loss. The Indians did not mount regimented cavalry charges, preferring instead to attack in waves, wage war from ambush, charge, retreat, hang low off the ponies and shoot from beneath the necks of their mounts. In short, fight as guerillas on horseback.

These tactics surely must have been befuddling to Custer. Add to this the fact that his men in the Seventh Cavalry were such poor soldiers, and that his promotion at such an early age and the subsequent coverage in the press of his almost every move had swelled his ego up like a hot air balloon, and the battle at Little Bighorn was inevitably going to be his great defeat. The press had also begun to report that Custer was whipping the Indians in battle everywhere he went and the general himself, some say, was beginning to believe what he read in the eastern papers and not the reality of the situation around him. When one examines the tactics used at Little Bighorn one has to wonder if Custer was in complete control of his mind that day, if perhaps he fell victim to some delusion of glory or grandeur. Or perhaps Little Bighorn was a suicide charge, the last hurrah that would make him a national hero forever. He was, after all, a romantic type.

PLATE 89:
WAR PARTY (1980),
38 x 50″
Collection
Mr. Anthony DeSantis

Sitting Bull, Crazy Horse and the other Sioux and Cheyenne chieftains survey Crook and his troops from a bluff overlooking the Powder River.

Several miles from the Little Bighorn, Custer ordered Major Reno to take half the column to the north end of the Indian encampment and mount a charge from that position, while he, Custer, would attack from the north end. The Indian encampment consisted of Oglalas, Hunkapas, San Arcs, Minneconjous, Black Feet Sioux, Brules and Santees (all bands of the Dakota Sioux) and some Yankatonias (Cheyenne), as well as some Blue Clouds (Arapaho), who were the least in number. To divide a few hundred poorly-disciplined cavalry troops against such overwhelming odds and expect to win shows a real lack of judgement, or sanity, on the part of General Custer.

My painting *Reno's Column* shows the major and his troops advancing on that day. Riding beside the major is a Crow scout. By setting this scene in a stand of long-dead trees, with their skeletal configurations, and patchy grass, I was able to heighten the sense of impending disaster. As in *Yellow Hair's End*, I made the standard of the Seventh a prominent part of the background.

Plate 90

Luckily for Major Reno and his troops, many of the Indian braves were out of camp on a buffalo hunt that day. When Reno led his men on an attack from the southern end, they were sent running by the Indians who were still in camp. Had all the braves been present, Reno and all of his troops would probably have perished that day also. As it was, they were severely routed and went running across the river. The survivors went charging up a narrow arroyo. (This account is related in pretty much the same way by survivors of Reno's column, and by the Indians.)

Custer, in the meantime, had charged the north end of the encampment. His attack was repelled and he retreated with his

PLATE 90:
RENO'S COLUMN (1969), 24 x 32"
Prudential Collection

*A Crow scout rides at the head of Major Reno's detachment
as the troops headed for Little Big Horn.*

men to the grassy ridge where he made his final stand. According to all accounts we have from the Indians, the Cheyennes were camped at the north end of the Indian enclave. However, and the Indians who have spoken of that day all tell it the same way, the first warrior to take off after the retreating bluecoats was Crazy Horse. At his side were two other young war chiefs: Kicking Bear and either Flying Hawk or White Bull of the Hunkapas. These chiefs were soon followed by about five hundred to seven hundred warriors from all the bands I just mentioned. The stories that white men tell, saying Custer was up against four to five thousand Indians, are just not true. Even Major Reno, in his report on the battle, stated that there were about eleven hundred "hostiles." These exaggerations probably stem from the fact that people of that time just did not want to believe that the "greatest" Indian fighter of all time was whipped by only a few hundred Indians.

When painting *Yellow Hair's End* I tried to capture what Custer must have felt in those final moments: the madness, the courage, the outrage, the realization that this was the end and to go down fighting was the only way. Also, by painting what amounts to a war-landscape portrait, I was able to emphasize the isolation of Custer, trapped not only on the knoll at Little Bighorn, but also trapped in the private hell of his own egotism and madness. The painting is above all a study in what can happen when you fully believe in yourself as a living legend. In spite of his egotism, his overrated reputation as a military strategist, his cowardly attack on Black Kettle and his band, there is something about General George Armstrong Custer that fascinates me to this very day.

Two other paintings deal not with the leaders of the battle that day, but with the "common soldiers" on both the Indian and the cavalry sides: *Desperate Leap* and *The Rescue.* In spite of the fact that my sympathies have always been with the Indians, I realized that there must have been camaraderie and friendship, and even heroism, among the troops of the Seventh Cavalry. *Desperate Leap* shows a man trying to help a fallen comrade. Clearly the attempt is futile. The soldiers are outnumbered almost two to one, as they were at Little Bighorn. Yet this man leaping from the horse chose to take his chances and do his best in spite of those odds. The painting is a statement on the nature of courage.

The Rescue shows a Cheyenne coming to the aid of a Sioux who has been shot from his pony. The difference in headdress points out the difference in tribe. The arrow sticking in the ground emphasizes the absolute chaos of the battle. Clearly this scene takes place on the fringe of the action, yet arrows are flying. I also wanted to emphasize the youthfulness of many of the braves who fought that day. The brave lying on the ground is a young man. Knocked from his horse, he tried to use his lance to keep his balance and broke the weapon, which lies in the lower right hand corner of the work. *The Rescue* also shows the Indian's riding prowess. Even though the Seventh was a cavalry unit, it was no match for these men who practically lived on their ponies almost from the time they were old enough to walk.

Victorious, a painting I consider one of my most

Plate 91
Plate 92

Plate 93

205

accomplished works, shows an Indian warrior just after Little Bighorn. The warrior has his hands raised towards the heavens; in one he holds a saber captured from a fallen cavalry soldier, while the other, empty hand symbolizes the emptiness of a victory that cost the lives of friends and relatives. The horse was also captured from the cavalry.

Everything in this painting, every detail, contributes to the whole. The dustiness and barrenness of the landscape symbolize the death and destruction the whites brought with them to the West. The close horizon created by the near hills surrounding the rider are reminders of the fact that, after the Little Bighorn, the horizons and frontiers that were left to the Indian had shrunk considerably.

THE AFTERMATH

A little more than a year elapsed before Crazy Horse brought his band in to the Indian Agency surrounding Fort Robinson. His people were starving because a bad winter and a dry summer had made the game almost disappear from the Black Hills. Plus, the stream of ever-increasing white men hunting for gold led Crazy Horse to the conclusion that neither he nor any other Indian would ever be able to defeat the invaders. It was a dejected, almost somnambulistic young chief who led his people to Red Cloud's Agency, as it was called.

Before taking his people in, Crazy Horse had received assurances that they would be fed and protected.

PLATE 91:
DESPERATE LEAP (1957), 24 x 36"
Prudential Collection

*Though my sympathies have always been with the
Indians, there was camaraderie, friendship and heroism
among the troops of the Seventh Cavalry.*

PLATE 92:
THE RESCUE (1959), 30 x 40″
Prudential Collection

The theme of Desperate Leap *is repeated
from the viewpoint of the Indian warriors.*

Black Elk says that in spite of these assurances the thirty year old chief looked wary, as though he knew what was going to happen.

The Indian Agency was patrolled by armed Lakota braves of Red Cloud's band who went by the name of "Indian police." Crazy Horse's band had dismounted and begun to mingle among the rest of the "Hangs-Around-The-Fort." Little Big Man, an Indian turncoat who now collaborated with the whites, led Crazy Horse into a log stockade, promising that the young chief would be given food and blankets to distribute among his people.

Once inside the stockade, Crazy Horse was seized and put into leg irons. He was paraded around in this manner, inside the stockade where the other Indians could not see what was happening, because they would probably have risen up and raised all sorts of havoc if they had. Various officers asked the young chief questions, which he could not answer because he did not understand English. They taunted him for awhile, then left him in the company of some enlisted men. Soon after, Little Big Man seized Crazy Horse by the arms and held him. One of the enlisted men then ran a bayonet through the Sioux who had defeated Custer. This is the way Crazy Horse died, butchered like a cow in a slaughter house, without a single chance.

It is probably quite likely that these enlisted men were acting under orders from the officers. A prisoner as important as Crazy Horse is not executed without some sort of command from those in charge.

*The cavalry horse and saber represent the Indian victory at Little Big Horn.
The surrounding hills and close horizon symbolize the closing-in of the white
man; the battle was won, but the war is almost lost.*

That night, Crazy Horse's father and two brothers climbed
the log walls of the stockade. Inside they knocked out the guard
and cut down the body of their chief from where it had been
strung up. It was probably the soldiers' intention to parade all of
Crazy Horse's followers before the corpse the next day.

His father and brothers escaped from the agency and took
the body of Crazy Horse deep into the Black Hills. There they
buried him, without ever telling anyone else exactly where.

After Little Bighorn, or Greasy Grass, as it should be called
since the Indians won, cavalry troops with cannon and Gatling
guns poured into the Black Hills to avenge Custer's death and to
free the land for the mining interests. General Crook led a
massacre against the encampment of Sitting Bull's people shortly
afterwards and the troops butchered sleeping women and
children while the men were out hunting.

The following spring Sitting Bull led his band, now down to a
few hundred, across the border into Canada. He immediately
contacted the authorities, after counciling with the chiefs whose
tribes had been living for years under British rule, and asked that
he be granted asylum under the Great White Mother, Queen
Victoria. Word was eventually sent to Ottawa. The matter was
taken under consideration.

In the meantime Sitting Bull settled down to a law-abiding
life. He had a bit of trouble for a while with some of the younger
men in his tribe. They were accused of crossing the border into
the United States to steal horses. Sitting Bull explained to them

PLATE 94:
SITTING BULL (1974), 24 x 30"
Prudential Collection

*This is Sitting Bull after the Battle of the Little Big Horn,
reflecting on the devastation of his dreams.*

that they must not do this again because the law of the Great White Mother forbade such action.

I find it very interesting that after the death of his mother, Sitting Bull sought refuge under the protection of another woman. It is as if he were listening to the spirit of his own mother.

In my study of *Sitting Bull Mounted* I show the chief alone and contemplative in the snowy reaches stretching across Canada. His coup stick has many feathers on it, but still he wears only the solitary eagle feather in his hair. He is thinking of his native land, longing to return yet wary, after so much betrayal, of the white man's assurances.

When Sitting Bull was finally granted permission to return to the Black Hills, a cavalry escort met him and his band at the border. The great chief was immediately clapped into irons and separated from the rest of the Sioux. He was taken to Fort Randall where he was imprisoned for the next six years. Once again, the white man had proved to the Indian that a promise was only good if it served the whites.

Eventually he was released to travel with *Buffalo Bill's Wild West Show*. When he finally returned, to live out his years with his people, it was to the Pine Ridge Reservation. There he lived in a shack miles away from the trading post that was the center of reservation activity. Ironically, his life ended in an assassination carried out by the Indian Police force. The greatest of all Sioux leaders was felled by blows delivered by fellow tribesmen who had come to believe that Sitting Bull was a menace to the existence of the people he had fought to protect.

"Peace"
Perillo ©80

8

Animals and Children

IN THE TWENTY EIGHT YEARS that I have been going out West to paint and draw and observe nature at its fullest, one thing has been uppermost in my mind—I want to paint for people. While I recognize the place in the art world for art historians, and the necessity of museums where art is preserved and cared for by specialists, I mainly paint paintings that are meant to be lived with. It has always been my belief that art is life-affirming. Nothing makes me happier than hearing from someone who has one of my paintings hanging in his home and is totally satisfied with it. What could possibly be a greater compliment to an artist?

Plate 96
Plate 95

Paintings like *Little Buffalo*, which shows a calf being followed by an adult buffalo, or *Magnificent Leap* with the cougar attacking the ram, are unadulterated paeans to the beauty of nature. They are meant to be enjoyed without having to strain the mind with theory and criticism.

Plate 99

I also often paint portraits of Indian children. Ever since my first trip to the Anderson Ranch, while I was in the navy, Indian children have seemed to me to be like little angels in dungarees. Recently I did a large painting—*The Mighty Hunter*—in which I explore this sentiment in an ironic sort of manner. The story here is simple—after having spent the day hunting, the boy has finally bagged his catch. It is sunset and the quiver holds one last arrow. By having the boy hold the goose over his shoulder I was able to give the sense of wings on the back of the child, though he is a scamp, as can be seen in his mischievous eyes. He is an angel with upside–down wings that are not really his. The depth of the sky and water in the background add a sort of heavenly quality to the piece. This is similar in nature to the early portraits I did of Indian children, before 1971. *Apache Princess,* with its panoramic background, is a good example of my treatment of this theme during those early years.

Plate 100

Some time ago I was represented by the Wally Findlay Gallery in New York City, and I was the first American artist, and first realistic painter, that that gallery ever handled. I did quite well with them and it was during this period that I took some time off to go to Italy. At the time I was looking for a new technique which I would employ in the *Companions* series I was planning to start after my vacation.

I found the technique in Tiepolo's murals on the ceiling in the Vatican Museum. When I saw them something clicked. These murals, which are filled with cherubs, reminded me of the Indian children who have inspired so many of my paintings. Whenever Mary and I visit the reservations, we take with us toys and clothes and sometimes I give the kids lessons on how to play baseball or how to box, boxing having been my own favorite sport when I was growing up. It still is my favorite sport, only now it is strictly from a spectator's viewpoint. Anyway, when I saw all those cherubs against the umber tones it became immediately clear to me that that is what I wanted to use for my *Companions* series. I have been an admirer of Tiepolo's since my student days. But seeing the murals in real life made me realize the depth and sense of roundness lent to a representation that uses these umber tones as background.

Plate 106

Arctic Shepherd, with the boy tending a herd of Dali rams, was an early attempt at fusing these tones into my work. I was still trying to give it a landscape effect, as is obvious by the sense of northern waters and sky in the painting. *Sand Storm*, a Plate 111 watercolor, is done in the same vein and shows an Apache boy wrestling with a spirited colt.

Plate 103
Plate 105
Plate 104
Plate 113
Plate 107

But it was in works like *Indian with Cougar*, *Arapaho Pony* and *Eskimo Daydream*, as well as *Portrait of Sitting Bull* and *Dignity*, that I began to feel totally at ease with this simple yet effective background. The painting in which I made this transition is titled *Up a Tree*. You can see the tree and the green leaves, yet the space behind the raccoon and child are devoid of landscape. I was finally able to see the strength simplicity would lend to this series.

Many of the paintings in the *Companions* series are sentimental in both mood and subject matter. That's because I am very sentimental about Indian children. Though the history of the treatment of the Indians in this country grieves me, it is in the children and in the future that I place my hopes. Also, I do

219

not believe that art must always come from a point of pain and suffering. I love to paint and these works show that, without apology.

In the *Companions* series I use the *trompe l'oeil* effect of having the eyes appear to be staring at you from every angle at which the painting is viewed. This adds to their effectiveness as works of art and also helps to drive home my point—the American Indian is not simply a part of history. There are Indians alive now and, while we cannot change the past, we can all work towards some better future. The eyes of these beautiful children remind you of that. People all over the world have seen these paintings and have them hanging in their homes. The knowledge of this gives me great pleasure. I want people to enjoy these paintings and live with them, and through living with them realize that there is always hope for the future, that life can always be better than it has been in the past. I think all of us want the world to be a better place. If my art helps in any little way to bring about that end, I will be happy. That, more than anything else, will be my reward.

May the Great Spirit
Smile on you
as long as the grass grows
and the water flows.

PLATE 95:
MAGNIFICENT LEAP (1975), 30 x 40″
Courtesy Empire Art Gallery, Empire, Colorado

A cougar is shown attacking a ram in the mountains of Colorado.

PLATE 96:
LITTLE BUFFALO (1966), 18 x 24"
Collection Russel Farrar

A cow watches over her calf.

PLATE 97:
BUFFALO (1969), 10 x 12″, pen and ink
Artist's Collection

*This drawing is the result of many hours of study
of the buffalo in their natural habitat.*

PLATE 98:
EAGLE SCOUTS (1976), 24 x 30″
Courtesy Images Gallery, Minneapolis, Minnesota.

*Here I depict a young warrior and an
eagle silhouetted against the Western sky.*

PLATE 99:
MIGHTY HUNTER (1980), 46 x 34″
Collection Mary Perillo

*Indian children seem to me to be like little angels in dungarees.
Here the wings of the captive goose serve as the wings of the angel.*

226

PLATE 100:
APACHE PRINCESS (1962), 30 x 24″
Courtesy University of New Mexico

Her staff is to remind her not to forget to attend
the sheep and goats that are her responsibility.

PLATE 101:
SPRING FAMILY (1975), 24 x 30″
Prudential Collection

A Canadian goose tends to her family
while a gander patrols in the background.

PLATE 102:
MIGHTY SIOUX (1978), 24 x 36″
Images Gallery, Minneapolis, Minnesota

The majesty of an Indian child is comparable
to that of the mighty cougar.

PLATE 103:
INDIAN AND COUGAR (1978), 24 x 30"
Collection Richard Cebelli
The background incorporates the influence of Tiepolo.

PLATE 104:
ESKIMO DAYDREAM (1971), 30 x 24"
Collection Charles Ancona

A young Eskimo boy and his dog.

PLATE 105:
ARAPAHO PONY (1979), 30 x 24"
Courtesy Small World Gallery, Scottsdale, Arizona

This is another attempt to create an effective landscape background using the colors of Tiepolo.

232

PLATE 106:
ARCTIC SHEPHERD (1976), 24 x 50″
Prudential Collection

*A twelve year old boy is shown tending
a herd of Dali sheep.*

PLATE 107:
UP A TREE (1978), 30 x 24″
Courtesy Small World Gallery, Scottsdale, Arizona

I strove for the strength and simplicity achieved by the absence of a landscape background.

PLATE 108:
HIS MAJESTY (1957), 25 x 37″
Collection Mr. and Mrs. John Buttermark

A lion is shown relaxing and enjoying his kingdom.

PLATE 109:
THE STALLION (1969), 24 x 32″
Collection George Awn

*While the anatomy of the horse escaped me in my early
paintings, the encouragement of William R. Leigh and
hard work now make a painting like this seem easy.*

PLATE 110:
THE WATERHOLE (1975), 24 x 32″
Collection Annette Perillo

*Modern day ranch horses are shown huddling
for warmth in the dead of winter.*

PLATE 111:
SANDSTORM (1951), 17½ x 21½″
Collection Mr. and Mrs. John Buttermark

An Apache boy wrestles with a spirited colt.

PLATE 112:
HIGH COUNTRY (1974), 30 x 24″
Collection Stephen Perillo

A cougar perches amidst the rocky crags.

239

PLATE 113:
DIGNITY (1977), 30 x 24"
Collection Mr. and Mrs. Kevin T. Burke

A variation on the Madonna and Child theme of Madre.

PLATE 114:
HER HIGHNESS (1975), 30 x 24"
Collection Michael Frost

A portrait of an Indian child in ceremonial dress, which signifies her coming of age whereupon she is given a name for life.

PLATE 115:
INDIAN GIRL (1978), 24 x 18"
Collection Bob Stanton

*Indian children have been a source of
inspiration for many of my works.*

PLATE 116:
LITTLE BUFFALO, SIOUX (1979), 16 x 20"
Courtesy Small World Gallery, Scottsdale, Arizona

Such paintings are unadulterated
paeans to the beauty of nature.

AFTERWORD

WHEN FIRST APPROACHED about writing this book with Gregory Perillo I was hesitant. I did not know the man and was only vaguely acquainted with his work. Soon, however, I took a ferry ride from Manhattan to Staten Island and visited the artist in his home. As anyone who has had the pleasure of meeting Perillo knows, he is as captivating, charming and disarmingly friendly a person as one is ever likely to meet. He exudes happiness and an enthusiasm that is contagious. The prospect of working on a book with him quickly became an enjoyable reality.

Perillo gave me a manuscript which he had written. Much of it needed only rearranging and minor editing to be included in this book. We also spent many hours going over his work, discussing it, dissecting it for content and meaning. Perillo showed me things about his work I might not otherwise have seen; and I hope and believe that I did the same for him. In short, the writing of the preceeding text was a truly collaborative effort.

In any collaboration there are disagreements. It is inevitable that the tastes and ideas of two people differ on some points. Perillo and I had ours. For example, on the matter of sculpture:

Perillo believes that sculpting is by nature a lesser art form than painting. I could not disagree more thoroughly.

This is not to say that Perillo denigrates or disregards the medium entirely. On the contrary, he recognizes the importance of sculpture in the context of his own work, as well as in the work of others. His attitude seems to stem from the fact that sculpting comes so easily to him, and something that is so easy cannot be taken as seriously as painting, according to Perillo. In spite of our disagreement on the subject, and his own attitudes regarding the medium, Perillo assures me that he intends to devote much of the year 1982 to producing more sculpture.

It should be obvious that, first and foremost, Perillo is a painter. He loves his work. Each day he rises at seven a.m. and goes down to his studio. He works there until later afternoon, clad only in pajamas. Evenings he often spends sketching out future paintings. His work is truly his life. I asked him at one point if he did not sometimes feel a desire to pick up and take off on a trip around the world. His answer was that if he did that, he would not be able to paint.

At this writing Perillo is involved in negotiations with a New York City gallery which will be the exclusive dealer of his major works. Also in progress are plans to establish on Staten Island a museum which will become the permanent home of a large collection of Perillo's work. I wish Perillo the best of luck in his involvement in these endeavors. He proved himself during and after the writing of this book to be one of the most magnanimous and gracious spirits I have ever met.

The weekend after the initial text was finished, I was married at the Explorers Club in Manhattan. A major portion of the Club's art collection is the display of a number of the paintings of William R. Leigh. Perillo and his lovely wife Mary attended the wedding and I was eager to see his reaction upon seeing so many of his old master's works. Perillo on the other hand had a surprise for my bride and me. He and Mary presented us with a bronze bas relief depicting a buffalo hunt. We were, needless to say, enthralled at the beauty of the piece and the generosity of the gift.

I am grateful for having had the opportunity to work with Gregory Perillo on the writing of this book. Few people are allowed the privilege of going through the body of an artist's work with the artist himself. I hope that this book shares that experience with the many people who know and love Perillo's art, and with those who are enjoying their first exposure to the work of an important Western artist.

Stephen DiLauro

LIST OF PLATES

BIOGRAPHY

1932.	Born Greenwich Village, New York City
1934.	Family moved to Staten Island
1937.	Attended P. S. 29
1945.	Attended McKee Vocational High School
1947.	Attended Pratt Institute
1949.	Enlisted in the Navy
1950.	Met William R. Leigh in Arizona
1951.	Married Mary Vendetti
	Attended School of Visual Arts while working in sweat shop
1954.	Annette Perillo born
1955.	Art Students League
	Job with U. S. State Department
1956.	Stephen Perillo born

EXHIBITIONS

ONE MAN SHOWS

1. Sailor Snug Harbor, 1960
2. Nahas Gallery, Brooklyn, N.Y., 1963, 1964, 1965
3. The Cradle Gallery, Turkey Creek, Colorado, 1966, 1967, 1968, 1971
4. G. Harvey Gallery, Austin, Texas, 1970
5. Wally Findlay Gallery, Madison Ave., N.Y.C., 1972, 1974
6. Wally Findlay Gallery, Palm Beach, Florida, 1973
7. Wally Findlay Gallery, Beverly Hills, Calif. 1973
8. Flemington Gallery of Fine Arts, N.J., 1977, 1978, 1979
9. Brielle Gallery, Brielle, N.J., 1978

10. Empire Art Gallery, Empire, Colorado, 1976, 1977, 1978, 1979, 1980, 1981
11. Delphi Art Center, Rapid City, South Dakota, 1977
12. Katalpa Horse Ranch, Mason, Mich., 1978, 1979
13. Images of the Old West, Minneapolis, Minn., 1977

GALLERIES

1. Chamisa Gallery, Box 1912, Taos, New Mexico
2. Flemington Gallery of Fine Arts, Flemington, N.J.
3. Gallery at Shoal Creek, Austin, Texas
4. Images of the Old West, Minneapolis, Minn.
5. Overland Trail Galleries, Jacobson, Wyoming, and Scottsdale, Arizona
6. Empire Art Gallery, Empire, Colorado
7. Pritshard Gallery, Houston, Texas
8. Meinhard Galleries, Inc., Houston, Texas
9. Griffin Gallery, Eureka Springs, Eureka, Arkansas
10. Wally Findlay Galleries, Inc., 17 East 57 Street, N.Y.C.
11. La Petite Gallery, Mandel, Norway
12. Texas Art Gallery, Dallas, Texas
13. Small World Gallery, Scottsdale, Arizona

PERMANENT COLLECTIONS

1. Pettigrew Museum, Sioux Falls, South Dakota—
    Chief Sitting Bull, Kit Carson
2. Denver Museum of Natural History, Denver, Colorado—*Chief Red Cloud*
3. University of New Mexico—*Apache Princess*

BIBLIOGRAPHY

Anderson, Harry H. "Cheyennes at the Little Big Horn." *North Dakota History* volume 27, number 2 (spring 1960)

Bates, Charles Francis. *Custer's Indian Battles.* Privately printed, Bronxville, New York (1936)

Beals, Frank Lee. *Real Adventures with American Plainsmen.* H. Wagner (1954)

Benteen, Frederick William. *The Custer Fight; Captain Benteen's Story of the Battle of the Little Big Horn.* Privately published by E. A. Brininstool, Hollywood, California (1933)

Berthrong, Donald J. *The Southern Cheyennes.* University of Oklahoma Press (1963)

Black Elk. *Black Elk Speaks.* As told to John G. Neihardt (Flaming Rainbow). Illustrated by Standing Bear. W. Morrow & Co. (1932)

Carson, Christopher. *Kit Carson's Own Story of His Life.* As dictated to Col. and Mrs. D.C. Peters. Edited and published by Blanche C. Grant, Taos, New Mexico (1926)

Custer, Elizabeth Bacon. *Following the Guidon.* University of Oklahoma reprint of 1890 edition (1966)

Custer, George Armstrong. *My Life on the Plains.* University of Oklahoma Press (new edition) (1962)

Fee, Chester Anders. *Chief Joseph, The Biography of A Great Indian.* Wilson-Erickson, Inc. (1936)

Flying Hawk. *Chief Flying Hawk's Tales.* Alliance Press (1936)

Geronimo. *Geronimo's Story of His Life.* With S.M. Barrett. Duffield (1906)

Hans, Frederick Malon. *The Great Sioux Nation.* M.A. Donohue & Co. (1907)

Hodge, Frederick Webb (editor). *Handbook of American Indians North of Mexico*, Volume One. First published, 1910, for U.S. Government. Greenwood Publishing (1969)

Hodge, Frederick Webb (editor). *Handbook of American Indians North of Mexico*, Volume Two. First published, 1910, for U.S. Government. Greenwood Publishing (1969)

Howard, Helen Addison. *War Chief Joseph.* The Caxton Printers, Ltd. (1941)

Johnson, Enid. *Cochise, Great Apache Chief.* Messner (1953)

Johnson, Willis Fletcher. *The Red Record of the Sioux.* Edgewood Publishing Company (1891)

Marquis, Thomas Bailey (interpreter). *A Warrior Who Fought Custer.* University of Nebraska Press (1957)

White Bull. *The Warrior Who Killed Custer.* Translated by James H. Howard. University of Nebraska Press (1968)

Windolph, Charles A. *I Fought with Custer.* C. Scribner's Sons, Ltd. (1947)

DATES OF ARTICLES IN NEWSPAPERS AND MAGAZINES

1. *Artist Depicts Rugged West.* Show World, Austin American Statesman. April 23, 1972.

2. Empire Magazine, Denver Post. Color centerfold, eight photographs. Sunday, August 8, 1971.

3. *Indian Portraits.* Staten Island Advance. June 15, 1975.

4. *Indians of the American West.* Greater Tom's River Recorder. April 11, 1973.

5. *Island Artist.* Staten Island Advance. May 8, 1967.

6. *Kit Carson.* Sioux Falls Argus Leader. November 29, 1966.

7. Palm Beach Illustrated Magazine. Full page, five black and white photographs. Sunday, March 25, 1973.

8. Palm Beach Life Magazine. Five page story, seven color photographs. June, 1973.

9. *Perillo's Indians.* Staten Island Advance. September, 1958.

10. Plate Collector Magazine. October, 1980.

11. *Recorder of the Redman.* Newark Sunday News. May 14, 1967.

12. *Red Cloud and the North American Indian Museum.* Marathon News of Florida. February, 1961.

13. Southwest Art Magazine. Five page story, six color photographs. June, 1976.

14. *The Better Side of the Indian.* Palm Beach Post. March 22, 1973.